PRAISE FOR *THORN*

"Bill Thorn is one of the finest men I have ever known. He is a beacon of virtue, honor, and true championship performance. I daresay there is no one in our history that has more in sheer volume of accolades, all honorably earned, and all taught with the most stringent codes of discipline, fair play, and team consciousness."

—BILL CURRY, NFL Player, Collegiate Football Coach, and ESPN Analyst

"I leaned on lessons from Coach Thorn, who always encouraged us to follow the path that would give us the opportunity to make the greatest positive difference in service to others."

—ANDREW CATHY, CEO, Chick-fil-A

"Bill Thorn stays motivated year in and year out but also keeps his body healthy enough to race every single year. That kind of consistent dedication is so inspiring."

—AMY CRAGG, Two-Time US Olympic Track and Field Athlete

"I knew early on that Coach Thorn was a tough guy. It didn't take us long to learn he was compassionate. He had an innate ability to get to know who you were as an individual and teach you to do the things you never thought you could do."

—JOHN TILL, PHD, Rear Admiral, US Navy Reserve, Retired

"A Coach Thorn athlete is not just a good runner; they are a good person, will give it their all, and are most respectful to their competitors, just like Coach Thorn was to all of us opposing coaches and teams."

—ANDY CARR, Events and Athlete Support, Atlanta Track Club

THE SCRAPPY, RELENTLESS, AND INSPIRING TRUE STORY OF LEGENDARY COACH BILL THORN

THORN

mascotbooks.com

Thorn: The Scrappy, Relentless, and Inspiring True Story of Legendary Coach Bill Thorn

For more information, please contact:
Mascot Books, an imprint of Amplify Publishing Group
620 Herndon Parkway, Suite 220
Herndon, VA 20170
info@amplifypublishing.com
Library of Congress Control Number: 2025909213
CPSIA Code: PRV0326A
ISBN-13: 979-8-89138-674-7

Printed in the United States

To Patty, Lynn, Cheryl, Bill Jr., and Terry—thank you for the countless hours you gave up with your husband and dad so that he could pour into the lives of thousands of athletes. Your quiet sacrifice and gift of time made it possible for all of us to be shaped by his coaching, his wisdom, and his relentless belief in us.

TABLE OF CONTENTS

TIMELINE OF COACH THORN'S LIFE

1930	William Jackson Thorn is born September 4 in Birmingham, Alabama.
1937–1945	Attended Pratt Grammar School.
1945–1949	Attended Ensley High School. In 1948, Bill's father passed away, and Bill began work at TCI.
1949	Attended Athens College in Athens, Alabama, on a football scholarship.
1950–1954	Attended Birmingham Southern College—physical education degree. Held his first paid coaching job at the West Hills YMCA.
1954	Bill and Patty married on June 11, and Bill graduated from Birmingham Southern. Bill and Patty moved to Atlanta, and Bill attended Emory University Seminary for one semester.
1955–1959	First full-time coaching job at Georgia Military Academy (now Woodward Academy). Taught English, American history, world history, economics, sociology, and American government and served as dormitory parent for the cadets. Assistant football coach and head basketball coach for four years. Bill and Patty's first child, Lynn, was born, followed by their second child, Cheryl, two years later.
1959–1969	Head Coach and Athletic Director at Headland High School in East Point, Georgia. Earned first state-level coaching award with the 1964 Headland High School boys' track team. Bill and Patty's first son, Bill Jr., was born, followed by their second son, Terry, four years later.
1970	Ran in the first Peachtree Road Race.
1971–1980	Established Thorn Realty as well as Coach's Construction. Bought and sold land, developed subdivisions, and supervised the construction of residential homes, vacation homes, commercial buildings, churches, and schools. Opened a tire store, Coach's Tires, in business for five years in College Park, Georgia.
1981–1986	Head Football and Track Coach at Colonial Hills Christian School in East Point, Georgia. Won his first state championship as Head Coach of the 1982 Colonial Hills football team.

1986–1988	Head Football and Track Coach and Athletic Director at Fayette Christian School.
1988–1991	Bill Thorn, Perry Duncan, and Eddie Waggoner met at Shoney's Restaurant in Fayetteville, Georgia, and began tossing around the idea of establishing a new Christian school. After much talk and prayer, Landmark Christian School was born. The fledgling school held its first classes in a renovated cabinet shop in Fayetteville, Georgia. Bill coached football, boys' track, and baseball and was Landmark's first Athletic Director.
1991	Landmark purchased the thirteen-acre Campbell High School campus thanks to savvy negotiating by Bill.
1994	Completed twenty-fifth Peachtree Road Race; inducted into the Peachtree Road Race Hall of Fame. Featured article in the October 1994 edition of *Runner's World* magazine.
1996	Official torch bearer for the 1996 Summer Olympics.
1997	Featured in the May edition of *Southern Living* magazine for completing his twenty-seventh Peachtree Road Race. Received the Judo Brown Award from the Atlanta Track Club for service to the sport and community.
1998	Landmark's track and football stadium is named after Bill Thorn. Landmark dedicated a stone monument on the walkway leading to the newly dedicated Thorn Stadium, which is a tribute to Coach Thorn's creed, "Hard Work, Given Time, Defeats Talent."
2000	Inducted into the Central Alabama Amateur Softball Hall of Fame.
2003	Inducted into the Georgia Track and Field / Cross Country Coaches Association Hall of Fame (GATFXCCA).
2004	Landmark girls' track team sets record at state championship for most points ever scored in a state meet with 162. Olympic torch bearer for the Athens, Greece, Olympics.
2005	June 12 is honored as Bill Thorn Day in Tyrone, Georgia.
2008	NFHS South Sectional Coach of the Year—Boys' Track and Field.
2012	Honorary Meet Director and Speaker for the Georgia Olympics.
2018	NFHS National Boys' Outdoor Track and Field Coach of the Year.
2019	Bill retires after coaching his 42nd state championship team.

2020	Inducted into the GACA Hall of Fame.
2023	Served as the Grand Marshal for the AJC Peachtree Road Race and officially retired from the race after crossing the finish line for the 53rd time. Becomes the only person to have their name engraved on the winner's cup trophy who did not win the event.
2024	Bill's biography is published on Wikipedia.
2026	Bill Thorn's biography is published.

FOREWORD

BY ANDREW T. CATHY

Coach Bill Thorn is a living legend—and with very good reason. As a coach for more than half a century, including thirty-five years at Landmark Christian School in metro Atlanta, he led 42 teams to championships and was named Coach of the Year 131 times. Along the way, he helped shape the character and faith of thousands of student-athletes. To me, as one of those former young people, Coach Thorn is more—much more—than a legend. In fact, throughout my life, I've been blessed to know him as a coach, mentor, colleague, and friend.

When I met Coach in the summer of 1990, I was twelve years old, on the cusp of sixth grade, and I was eager to play football. At the time, Landmark didn't have a middle school team, just varsity and junior varsity.

I should mention here that I was never a big kid. So not only was I young and inexperienced, but I was also small, perhaps the smallest one out there, facing off against some guys twice my size. Even so, with Coach looking on, I couldn't help but try as hard as I could.

From the start, two things were clear about Coach Thorn. First, he expected us to always give our best effort, whether we were doing drills, working out, or scrimmaging. Second, he expected us to put in the work necessary to do our best. And trust me, we worked hard!

Our practices were tough, with lots and lots of running. Some players couldn't see past the grueling workouts, which routinely pushed us to our limits. Most of us, however, eventually caught the vision of what he was doing, and we pushed through, becoming stronger as individuals and as a team.

When I was in eighth grade, I joined the track team. In both football and track, Coach Thorn focused heavily on conditioning and teaching us the fundamentals through hard work and repetition.

We learned a great deal from the way Coach ran practices. We also learned from what he said about the keys to success, both on the field and off. To be sure, Coach talked to us a lot, often taking an hour or more at the end of practice to pour into us with his quotes, lessons, and acquired wisdom. As you might guess, practices rarely ended at the posted time.

As a high school athlete, I learned so much from Coach. He taught me—like countless others—the importance of hard work, preparation, dedication, and giving our best effort. And he did so not only through words but also through action. Indeed, he faithfully modeled the winning ways he taught us, always putting in the work to lead us well.

Coach would go to great lengths, for example, to prepare for upcoming opponents. In those preinternet days, this was done the old-fashioned way, with lots of shoe leather, phone calls, and scouting reports. For the state track meet, we would arrive early so he could study the times of other athletes. From this data, he would develop extensive scenario plans and strategies.

Coach Thorn alongside high school football player Andrew Cathy, Landmark Christian School

In addition, Coach took the time and made the effort to create individual development plans and workout schedules. He understood we were all different, all unique in our talents, capabilities, and weaknesses, and pushed us to levels we didn't think were possible. And he knew developing each of us required individual attention and planning. This leadership lesson will stay with me always.

After graduating college, I had the opportunity to return to Landmark as a business teacher and coach, making good on a promise I'd made to myself as an eighth-grader. As you might suspect, Coach played a big role in inspiring my interest in serving and helping shape young people.

For two years, I taught at Landmark while coaching football and track. By then, Coach had retired from football, but he continued to shepherd the track team. This meant I got to work under him as a fellow coach. Right away, he gave me real opportunities to lead, and I learned firsthand the value of developing others through delegation and trust.

While I thoroughly enjoyed teaching and coaching, in time, I would feel the pull to enter the family business of Chick-fil-A, founded by my grandfather S. Truett Cathy and later led by my dad, Dan T. Cathy.

Coach Bill Thorn, Coach Andrew Cathy, and Coach Roby Ross, alongside the 2005 Landmark State Champions Girls' Track Team

Even in this decision, I leaned on the lessons from Coach Thorn, who always encouraged us to follow the path that would allow us to make the greatest positive difference in service to others.

I knew that, for me, this would be through Chick-fil-A, and I joined the business as a restaurant operator in 2005.

When my wife, Mandy, and I were married in 2007, I asked Coach to serve as one of my groomsmen. It was a profound honor for me to have this man, who had done so much for me and meant so much to me, stand with me as we took our vows.

I will be forever grateful for the examples Coach Thorn set for me as a coach, servant leader, husband, and person of faith. As a Christian, he has loved and served God and other people with humility, compassion, and faithfulness for decades—and he continues to do so.

Today, when I think about Coach Thorn, I'm reminded of a passage from the concluding chapter of 2 Timothy:

I have fought the good fight. I have finished the race. I have kept the faith. Now there is in store for me the crown of righteousness, which the Lord, the righteous Judge, will award to me on that day—and not only to me but also to all who have longed for his appearing.

—2 Timothy 4:7–8, NIV

Like so many others whose lives and faiths have been shaped by Coach Bill Thorn, I am delighted by the publication of this wonderful book, which provides all those who come across it—both now and in the future—with the opportunity to learn from his life, his experiences, his wisdom, and his walk with God.

—Andrew T. Cathy, CEO, Chick-fil-A

Andrew Cathy alongside Bill at the Bill Thorn Gala celebration, March 2023

INTRODUCTION

BY JILLIAN BROADDUS

Any attempt to chronicle the life of Coach Bill Thorn in a mere biography would only serve to touch upon the surface of his remarkable journey. He has lived a "Forrest Gump-type" existence, marked by extraordinary accomplishments and quiet, profound influence. He has carried the Olympic torch twice, has triumphed over prostate cancer, and stands as the sole individual to have completed fifty-three consecutive Peachtree Road Races.

His coaching career spans six decades, during which he led thousands of athletes, securing a record-setting forty-two state titles across five distinct sports, often guiding underequipped teams to championship victories. He has been honored as Coach of the Year 131 times, mentored 173 individual state champion athletes, and has been inducted into four separate Halls of Fame. Beyond athletics, he founded a high school; managed successful real estate, construction, and tire businesses; and built a life alongside his wife of seventy years, Patty.

However, the true measure of his legacy lies not in a list of accolades, but in the "Thornisms" he imparted—lessons concerning goal setting, persistence, and dedicated, hard work that shaped his life and continue to guide those he coached, mentored, or encountered. These lessons now extend to you, the reader.

As we endeavored to gather memories and stories from the lives Bill Thorn touched, the challenge was not finding material, but rather determining where to conclude. Through website submissions, social media commentary, phone calls, video interviews, casual conversations, newspaper articles, online accounts, and stories shared during laps around his neighborhood during his fifty-third and final Peachtree, it became evident that there was no shortage of content.

Moreover, certain themes consistently emerged: tales of undersized, underequipped, underdog teams defying expectations, stories of resourceful training in challenging environments, and narratives of hard work overcoming talent. Behind these recurring stories were insights into why Bill consistently achieved success, built cohesive teams, and generated momentum from humble beginnings. These were tales of a leader who commanded respect through his own steadfast example, a man who openly expressed his faith, and a coach who valued effort and praised consistent dedication.

Coach and Jillian at the Bill Thorn Gala

We encountered stories of athletes who followed his example into coaching, individuals who pursued unconventional paths to success, and those who named children and businesses in his honor. We found accounts of people who overcame adversity by remembering Bill's example.

Ultimately, we recognized that the central question was not how to properly tell Bill Thorn's story, but whether it could be fully told at all. No array of adjectives or "Thornisms" could encapsulate a life spanning nine decades. While we can describe specific actions—a sixty-year-old man working on showers or building a house—we cannot fully convey the heart driving those actions, the unseen effort, or the memories he modestly withholds.

Thus, a single book cannot fully capture Bill Thorn's story. His legacy is woven into the lives he influenced, the minds he shaped, and the generations he transformed. We hope that the recounted tales, interspersed quotes, and evidence of his impact provide insight into the character of Bill Thorn. Because, as he said, "There are a lot of characters. Most people are characters. It's about good character." And he is about as good as they come.

A NOTE FROM BILL THORN

Here I am, at the age of ninety-four years old, reflecting on the years behind me and everything that's happened. *Why is this book being written about me?* It's a good question. In fact, it's one that I've been stewing on during this entire process.

A lot of this is a mystery to me. *What's all the attention for? Am I an oddball? Do I really do things that differently?* I guess the answer must be *yes*.

Coach Thorn at William J. Thorn Stadium, Landmark Christian School, 2019

Chuck Cusumano thought so, too, and tried to start this book in 2016. However, the timing was not right. Now that I am officially retired from coaching, and Chuck has the staff to pull off such a project, he and Lauren McGuire have teamed up to convince me to tell my life story. To me, my life has been a simple one—so I'll try to keep myself out of it as much as I can!

The only thing you can know about your influence on people is what they come back and tell you. Looking back on all of this, the book has stirred up a lot of things. First off, I didn't have any idea of my impact on all of you—the contributors to this book! Hearing and seeing the stories we created together helped me better see my role in all of this. So thank you all for sharing your words, pictures, thoughts, and memories—some of which I didn't recall until I heard them from you!

And secondly, witnessing how many of you have become successful in your own respective fields of endeavors has made me even more grateful to the Lord for allowing me the opportunity to work and coach so many lives. I didn't have to; I got to!

In my coaching career, every place I went was different, and everything had to be looked at with a fresh perspective. I had to figure out what was suitable for each new individual and team I was coaching. When it comes to sharing wisdom or things learned, it feels similar to that same challenge. I want something to resonate with everyone, but everybody learns and understands things differently; we all have different backgrounds and experiences and think of "wisdom" in different ways.

The pressure of that can feel overwhelming, especially when you think about all of the things you *could* say or all of the stories you *could* share.

So if I had to break it down, I'd say this: More than anything, I hope that those who read my book will have a better relationship with the Lord after reading it. I've been looking back through the years of each place and person who was important in my own life, and every moment of it points back to the Truth. So I hope whoever reads this book sees the Truth in it. Because to me, the Truth is the most important thing I can talk about.

I used to open up a lot of days at practice by reminding every athlete what all this was really about. First, it's about God's Truth. Coming to know Jesus Christ is everything, and I have been blessed in my marriage to Patty Thorn, who is sold out to Jesus Christ in every area of her life. She led me to the Lord slowly, encouraging me to listen to those who were teaching about the Lord. God's promise is all we need.

But it's also about the Truth of honesty, good character, and sticking to something, even when it's hard. It's about not giving up.

I want everyone to know that you can keep going. Those are words that you first have to know—but more importantly, you have to do something about them too. It takes work, effort, and consistency.

Work *works*!

Enjoy *your* stories. Enjoy the memories. I had no idea at the time that it would all add to something like this. If you put in the work and take time to invest in others, your life can add up to immeasurably more than you thought!

Thank you to all who gave me the opportunity to coach you!

—Bill Thorn, "Coach"

Thornism\ **thorn.is.m** (noun) A sentence, phrase, or word used by Coach Bill Thorn to *repetitively* drive home a point, make a statement, or to be used as an answer to a question.

Hard work, over time, defeats talent or takes talent to a higher level.

When it's hard to run—run hard.

When it's too tough for others . . . it's just right for us.

It's only for those who are here.

It's only for those who will do it.

Rain or mud Sweat or blood, the Lone Ranger's gonna ride!

If it were easy, everybody would be doing it.

Winners find a way.

If you think you are beaten, you are.

A good disposition is important; all great players have it.

He who won't be advised can't be helped.

"Play the game squarely" is one rule that will never be revised.

Your teammates keep your opponents off your neck.

Quitters never win, and winners never quit.

When you become complacent is when others have beaten you.

First things first, and first things right.

If you've done it before, it's still there.

ONE

"YOU CAN HAVE ANYTHING YOU WANT IN LIFE, SO LONG AS YOU CAN PAY FOR IT"

—J. P. THORN

A LIFE DEFINED BY GRIT, toughness, and determination rarely blooms from a soft entrance to the world. The lives of men like Bill Thorn—whose ways are set in iron, whose intentions are intense, whose faith in the Lord remains unshaken in the wildest of circumstances—often start and continue in an environment gripped by trial. For many determined men who make their way in the world the way Bill does, their beginning moments and their formative years are punctuated by hard lessons and complicated circumstances. Bill, born in the beginning days of the Great Depression, was no exception.

However, Bill's story goes beyond the circumstances thrust upon him. Bill's story is one of faith and of sharing God's love with all those whose lives he molded and influenced throughout his ninety-four years. Bill's story, part of a much greater story, continues to be written. It branches out through the lives he touched and flows from the life-impacting lessons he taught.

And like all great stories, Bill's has a captivating beginning—a beginning that sets the stage for the scrappy, relentless, and inspiring story of Bill Thorn . . .

Growing up in the early 1930s was a unique upbringing for any American.

Once wealthy men and family breadwinners found themselves as broken shadows of their former selves. Once powerful titles and impressive accolades now meant nothing. Everyone was equal when standing in line waiting for a meager meal handed out by government welfare to fend off ever-increasing starvation. Some chose to leave their families behind, riding the rails from town to town in search of money to send home. "Brother, can you spare a dime?" became a common phrase as makeshift neighborhoods known as Hoovervilles—a nod to the leadership that seemed to turn a blind eye to the deteriorating economic conditions sweeping the country—popped up like weeds for the homeless and impoverished. Some situations were so grave that children were given up for adoption—a lesser evil than the threat of starving at home.

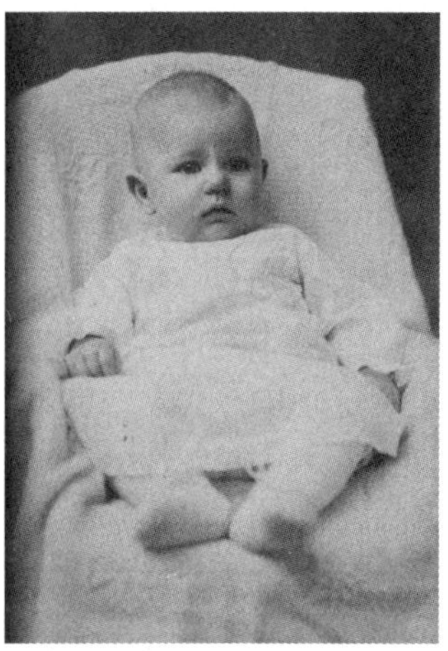

William J. Thorn, ca. 1930

Radio shows, comics, and a child's robust imagination provided the main sources of entertainment for the era and often served to reflect the sentiment of the times. "Little Orphan Annie"—known today for being the bright-eyed, red-headed girl singing confidently about "Tomorrow"—was born from a comic strip by Harold Gray, in which he depicted "a comfortless world, vaguely sinister, [filled with people] nearly paralyzed with fear and apprehension." Annie was drawn with blank eyeballs, symbolic of the mood of an uncertain and unpromising climate.

The times may have seemed the least ideal to contemplate starting a family. However, just a few months after Black Monday in 1929, Edna and Jackson Perry (J. P.) Thorn learned they would be bringing a child into the precarious new world. On September 4, 1930, in Birmingham, Alabama, they welcomed a son, William Jackson Thorn, who would be the eldest of five children in the Thorn family.

Bill's father worked as a barber, while Bill's mother tended to all aspects of the home. For the first few years of Bill's life, the family scratched out a scant living while bouncing around through numerous rental homes. Noticing the family's continual struggles, a relative on Bill's mother's side, Aunt Mattie, invited the Thorn family to come and live with her and her own mother, "Grandma Miller," in 1935 when Bill was five years old.

Aunt Mattie

A single, hardworking woman, Aunt Mattie proudly owned a small but cozy one-room home at 302 Avenue V, in Pratt City, Alabama, five miles northwest of downtown Birmingham. As Bill describes it, Pratt City was an industrial area as well as a cultural melting pot. The Tennessee Coal, Iron and Railroad Company (TCI) maintained a firm foothold in the area, attracting an assortment of people, including a large population of immigrants from Italy, Greece, and Syria. For Bill and his family, Pratt City represented the chance at stability and the opportunity to settle into a "forever" home. It also represented an opportunity for Bill's father to attract a steady stream of customers from the plentiful TCI employees looking for a skilled barber.

Bill and younger sister Martha-Ann, ca. 1935

However, this opportunity was only possible with the gracious assistance of Aunt Mattie. An accomplished seamstress at Kessler's—a brick-front, four-story, 14,000-square-foot department store with a pink-and-black granite-and-brass floor—she was well known for her exceptional craft among "people with money." Through working at one of the largest and highest-end department stores for

Martha-Ann, Edna, and Bill Thorn on the porch of 302 Avenue V, September 1937

women's clothing in Birmingham, Aunt Mattie was sought out by Birmingham's elite clientele and frequently received large tips for her beautiful handiwork. This extra income helped Aunt Mattie provide a home for the growing Thorn family, which now included younger sister Martha-Ann and little brother Bobby.

As the Thorn family grew, so did Aunt Mattie's house on Avenue V. As Bill describes it, when more space was needed, a tree from the yard was chosen, cut down, and used as the foundation for another room. The cramped house soon transformed into a two- . . . three- . . . four- . . . five- . . . six- . . . and finally, a seven-room home, complete with a back porch. This gradual expansion provided enough space for the Thorn family, Aunt Mattie, and Grandma Miller to settle into their multigenerational living in Pratt City.

Bill's school photo, 1939

Growing up as the eldest son, Bill was expected to contribute heavily to the family's chores. Dependable and trustworthy, Bill was given a dollar and a quarter every Thursday, carried in the watch pocket of his jeans, to buy chicken feed for the leghorn ("leggern") chickens his father raised in a backyard coop. Leghorns were busy and smart birds, used by the Thorn family to provide meat and eggs for their own table, as well as a means of income or way to barter with people in town. In addition to buying the feed for the chickens, Bill was responsible for fending off—with a BB gun or .22 rifle—the field rats and "pretty big" gophers responsible for stealing the eggs and killing the chickens.

Outside of caring for the chickens, Bill aided his mother and sister with the weekly washing. The family owned an "Easy washer," which utilized metal upside-down cups, like plungers, that created turbulence to clean the clothes as they moved in an up-and-down rhythm. Martha-Ann was tasked with wringing and hanging the clothes while Bill was charged with the preceding job: placing two tubs in the proper location on the back porch. Without a water heater in the home, Bill would heat water on the stove to pour in the tub to provide the first rinse for the clothes and linens and to take a bath every Saturday.

Bill and Martha-Ann playing with goats as Edna watches

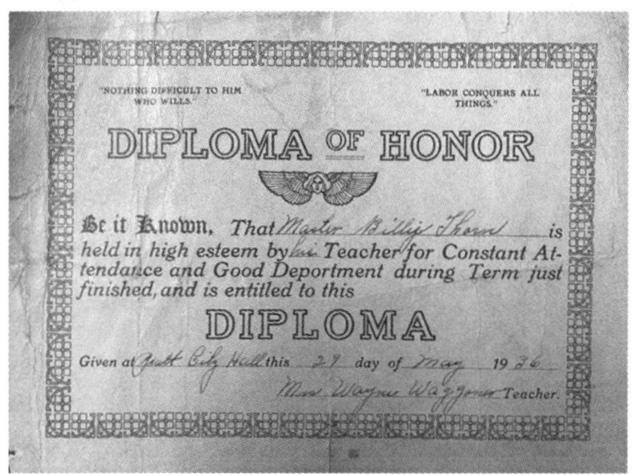

"NOTHING DIFFICULT TO HIM WHO WILLS." "LABOR CONQUERS ALL THINGS."

DIPLOMA OF HONOR

Be it Known, That Master Billy Thorn is held in high esteem by his Teacher for Constant Attendance and Good Deportment during Term just finished, and is entitled to this

DIPLOMA

Given at [illegible] this 29 day of May 1936

Mrs Wayne Waggoner Teacher.

Award for Good Attendance and Deportment for Master Billy Thorn, May 1936

Although a workhorse for the family, Bill also admits that he had ways of "slipping" around on chores to get them done faster so he could get back to playing. As the kindling cutter for the family, Bill devised a ruse to make the kindling pile appear larger than it was by flipping a peach basket upside down and stacking the kindling around it instead of filling the basket itself. Aware that a whipping would likely follow if his system was discovered, he diligently checked the pile daily to ensure no parts of the peach basket began to show, ensuring that his facade was never discovered.

In his limited free time between school, athletics, chores, and small jobs at A&P Grocery and Cale's Drugstore, Bill spent afternoons swimming with friends in a murky swimming hole outside of Pratt City. Snake heads popped out of the water like whack-a-moles on all sides of the boys, which they "just didn't pay attention to," mistakenly assuming snakes couldn't bite underwater. He enjoyed the autonomy to run around town but dreamed of having something that would increase his independence: a bicycle.

Aunt Mattie, date unknown

Growing up, Bill was very close with his Aunt Mattie. Every day he would anxiously await her arrival after her shifts at Kessler's, and excitedly yell, "Aunt Mattie, ain't you got me anything?" as he saw her rounding the corner, walking home from the streetcar line. As he would run up to her, she'd reach in her pocket for a few spare coins to spoil her oldest nephew. This dependable allowance, along with his pocket change earned from stocking shelves or delivering prescriptions, served Bill well as he grew up under her roof, but it was never quite enough for Bill to afford his dream bicycle.

However, Bill's dream finally came true on Christmas Day of 1940 when he was ten years old. Under the fresh-cut tree and glinting ornaments sat a bike Aunt Mattie had bought used from a relative. Bill was ecstatic; as an almost-teenage boy, two wheels finally gave him his very first taste of freedom that he had dreamed of for so long.

Although he loved his new gift and the freedom it brought him, Bill's bike stowage at home proved to be rather sloppy. Wherever he rode, he finished his route by cycling home on Avenue V and tossing his bike, handlebars first, into a cloud of dirt in the front yard. His father, who made it a habit of parking at an angle, askew from the driveway, wasn't happy with

Bill's bike placement blocking his parking space.

More than once, Bill admitted, he got a lecturing.

"Son," his father finally said one evening, "I'm telling you for the last time: If you put that bicycle there again, I'll run it over."

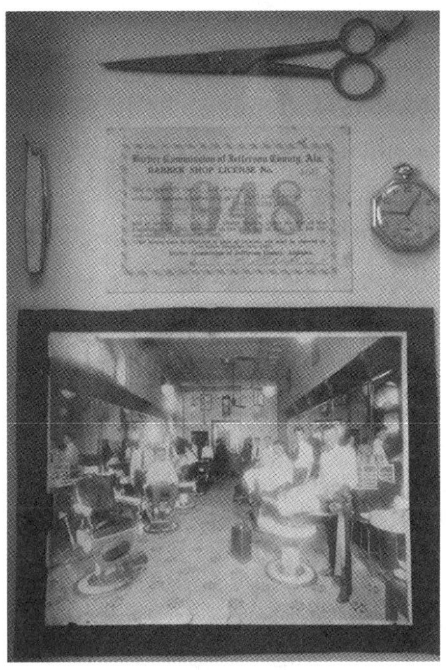

J. P. Thorn's Barbershop, ca. 1948

Bill's parents, although loving toward their family, displayed their love in very different forms. A descendant of Irish immigrants who arrived in South Carolina but relocated to Alabama via covered wagon trains, Edna largely "went along with everything" and never questioned or "spoke up about much." Bill's father was very different. A product of a tough upbringing in a hand-built house on Cotton Gin Road in Beaverton, Alabama, J. P. Thorn was a serious man who "said what he meant and meant what he said." He'd made it a point to tell the teachers and principal at Bill's school, "If you have any problems with my son, let me know, because he's going to have some with me at home." J. P.'s way of thinking was born from trust; he trusted that the authority figures knew what they were doing and trusted they'd handle situations appropriately. He'd also been known to give Bill whippings—some Bill "surely deserved," and some (he claims) he didn't. However, when it came to his father's threat on Bill's prized possession, Bill heard his words but, well, "didn't take it in right."

So the next time Bill bounded into the yard to ride his bike, he found it bent, bruised, and battered, a casualty of his father's not-so-empty promise that he'd run it over if Bill didn't stow it right. Both wheels were twisted, rendering the bike unrideable and leaving the metal bent unnaturally in a sad pile amid the dirt.

Bill, distraught, lugged the beaten bike to the back of the house, where Aunt Mattie found him crying. Bill knew it was up to him to fix his bike without much money in his pocket beyond the spare coins Aunt Mattie would toss him on her commute home.

Fortunately, a neighbor named Mr. Bowers owned a bicycle repair shop around the corner, on Avenue U. Aunt Mattie took Bill's bike, with a request to do "anything needed to make it look good."

Once it was fixed, Bill learned several important lessons. One, take good care of the things you have. Two: When you say you are going to do something, you do it. And three: Take his father at his word.

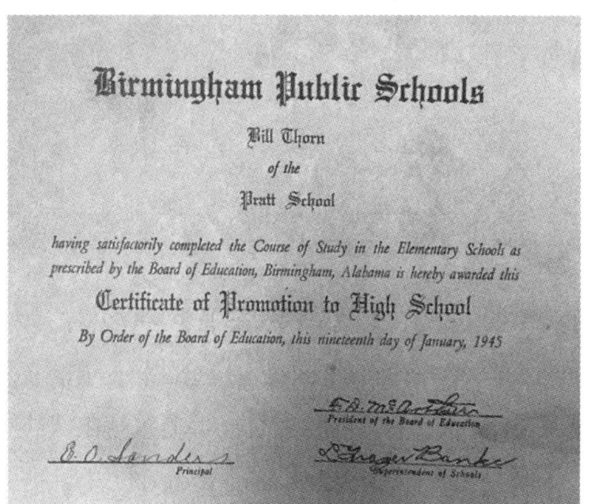

Birmingham Public Schools

Bill Thorn

of the

Pratt School

having satisfactorily completed the Course of Study in the Elementary Schools as prescribed by the Board of Education, Birmingham, Alabama is hereby awarded this

Certificate of Promotion to High School

By Order of the Board of Education, this nineteenth day of January, 1945

President of the Board of Education

Principal

Superintendent of Schools

Bill's promotion certificate to high school, 1945

Despite a modest childhood, J. P. eventually built a successful three-chair barbershop on Avenue U in Pratt City, at a crossroads along the streetcar line. The barbershop stood surrounded by two drugstores on either side of the tracks and served as one of the few places with electric clippers, although J. P. still preferred the more traditional way of cutting hair—what some people called a "scissor and comb guy." It took J. P. longer to cut a head of hair, but the quality and appearance of the end product were why people continued to come. J. P. took pride in everything he did and was very meticulous—traits Bill would carry throughout his life.

His father was careful with his tools—cleaning them daily and trusting Bill to clean up the shop. Bill often went straight from school to the barbershop, where he'd sweep hair from the floor, rinse tools according to his father's instruction, and—once his father had gone home—goof around with friends. Bill's friends liked to join him for afternoons at the shop, but Bill had to come up with reasons for them to be there; from needing shaves to needing haircuts, Bill found ways for his friends to accompany him until closing time. They'd crank up the leather chairs and twirl one another around until the spinning would completely lay them out, or leave them staggering helplessly, dizzy-headed around the floors. Bill would lock up for the night, knowing his antics wouldn't go unnoticed: "You didn't have to tell J. P. You just waited till he opened up the next morning. He already knew."

As the years passed and Bill entered his teenage years, the Second World War broke out. Eager to join the fight, Bill lied about his age and snuck down with friends to the Birmingham post office to try to enlist. "Boys," they were told by enlistment officers, "y'all need to get home and tend to your chores."

Hudson Terraplane advertisement from the magazine Country Gentleman

However, J. P. Thorn was able to join the war effort—albeit in a different capacity. Putting his barbering tools on hold, J. P. made extra money by working for the War Department at the Birmingham airport. The family car was critical in his earning the job, as the government was searching for someone capable of loading their car with three or four extra people to bring to work with them every day. So with a 1937 Hudson Terraplane—an inexpensive yet powerful vehicle, sturdy like a tank and teeming with steel—J. P. won the role, plus some extra rations for gasoline.

Outside of his ability to shuttle employees to work, he served as the shift manager and crew overseer with the Betchel McComb company, monitoring B-24s as they came in from Willow Run out of Detroit, Michigan.

Although proud to serve in the war effort, it was during this time that

J. P. started having trouble with his lungs. A deep cough eventually led to unstoppable hacking fits, while weakness began consuming his body. Although in failing health, after the war ended, J. P. returned to his only other way of making income—cutting hair.

Bill was a teenager at this point and knew that his father was getting sick. However, he realized that his father must be getting seriously ill as he stopped doing the one thing he loved more than almost anything: fishing. J. P. fished for sport, food, and camaraderie on Lake Purdy, along with a close friend who owned another barbershop in Birmingham. Bill would join, tasked with driving the boat. Bill learned how to avoid hitting the dinghy with the paddle, and how to twist and guide it in a way to get the boat cruising evenly, while watching his father create his own flies with squirrel tails and invent his own ways of designing fishing lures. But Bill also learned the unspoken nuances of successful fishing: Bill's father was strict and precise in every detail—from determining the right position to bite, to dictating the quiet ambience of the atmosphere. His fishing hobby was a lesson in discipline, and Bill watched him silently and copied his protocols out on the water. For the last thirty minutes of each trip, Bill was allowed to take the reins, throwing the fly rod in search of white perch, also known as "crappies."

When his days on the lake became fewer and further between, Bill's concern for his dad's health began to grow.

J. P., Edna, Bobby, Martha-Ann, Bill Thorn, ca. 1945

He was soon diagnosed with tuberculosis, and later on with diabetes, and was a "guinea pig" at the time for new drugs on the market. Streptomycin wasn't yet used to treat tuberculosis, so the chosen method of treatment was grueling: If a patient could take air in, they'd collapse the lung and let it heal. If they couldn't—which was J. P.'s case—they opted to cut into the back to remove all traces of the infection inside. For Bill's father, the procedure cut every rib out of the left side of his body in an effort to rid the infection—to no avail.

J. P. spent the last two years of his life from 1946 to 1948—during Bill's teenage years—at a tuberculosis sanatorium on Lakeshore Drive, not far from Howard College (now known as Samford University). Bill and his father saw the end in sight, and both knew of the impending worry of their family's loss of its only income stream. The barbershop was still up and running, entrusted to the care of one of J. P.'s employed barbers, but no one was sure what would eventually happen to the business with the passing of J. P.

Bill was the last one to see his father alive. He spent the night with him at the sanatorium, just before he died on Sunday, May 22, 1948, at two in the afternoon. At just seventeen years old, Bill found himself the head of his family.

In J. P.'s final months, Bill thought of something his dad said often. Whether it was regarding his broken bicycle or a shiny new toy, Bill's father would remark, "Son, you can have anything you want in life, so long as you can pay for it."

Bill knew he had to figure out what he wanted to do with his life, to provide for his mother, continue raising his siblings, and save up for the life he wanted. He just didn't know what that path looked like quite yet.

TWO

"IF YOU THINK YOU ARE BEATEN, YOU ARE" —THINKING, WALTER D. WINTLE

IT'S THE BIG, life-changing moments that often tell us who we are: how we react, what plans we make, and how we pick up the pieces of things that shatter around us. Those are the things that tell everyone, as well as ourselves, about our priorities, our character, our grit, and our faith.

Bill's came when his father died, just as he was finishing high school and stepping out into the world.

Suddenly, every what-if, every possible route for his life, and every opportunity in front of him looked different than it had in the weeks before his father passed. After all, it wasn't just about Bill and which path he'd take anymore; it was about supporting his family, financially and emotionally, while navigating the journey of figuring out who he was supposed to be and what he was supposed to do with his life.

Bill's high school graduation photo, Ensley High School, 1949

Despite his father's insistent and not-too-discreet attempts to persuade Bill into barbering, Bill "never had any intention of taking over the business." Instead of totally closing the shop, Bill, Edna, and a former employee of his father's worked out an agreement to keep the shop up and running, with Edna maintaining the licenses and the former employee managing the day-to-day operations. With the shop at least temporarily settled, Bill decided to join the ranks of what many of his friends in Pratt City were destined for: work at the Tennessee Coal, Iron and Railroad Company. And just one short month after high school graduation, Bill became a TCI employee.

The financial opportunities at the company seemed like the most logical choice. As the second largest steel producer in the US and the primary employer of men in northern Alabama, TCI was booming. As the economic backbone of the town, everyone (and everything) became shaped by it. So much so that Bill recalled, "The air was so full of soot that clumps the size of golf balls needed to be swept off the porch." While happy to be employed with a source of income for the family, Bill soon found the work at TCI to be backbreaking, "terrible," and unfulfilling.

Bill with his mother

Bill trudged through his days at TCI "sucking up" the work like "everyone else," scratching out a meek living for his family. While his future looked bleak, a happenstance meeting with a random man one day at TCI changed the whole trajectory of Bill's life . . .

That man was Jim Hodges, who was working in the same area that Bill was. As they started talking and telling each other about their lives, Bill learned that Jim was still in high school at Fairfield High and was a star lineman on the football squad; however, Jim had very different plans than Bill following graduation. Jim had recently taken a trip up to Athens College (now Athens State University) in Athens, Alabama, to try out for the football team. Jim performed well and had been offered a football scholarship for the following spring.

After hearing Jim's story, Bill immediately knew that he wanted to do the same thing.

Bill had been a multisport athlete at Ensley High School, participating on the school's baseball, basketball, and football teams. However, he wasn't necessarily the school's "star" athlete. Bill made the football team only after sneaking out of the house for tryouts to avoid the wrath of his father—who discouraged the sport—and had never been the coach's first pick to start. Admittedly, most of Bill's playing time came amid massive upsets—part of a last-ditch, "why-not-let-him-play" mindset. However, Bill had some things many of the athletes didn't have: a winning outlook, unwavering dedication, and a belief that he was never beaten, no matter how bad the circumstances seemed. But how could Bill get a college football coach to see that, let alone offer him a scholarship for it?

Bill knew somehow, someway, he had to get to Athens College and talk to the coach himself.

Alongside a friend, John Shafer, and completely unannounced, Bill hitchhiked his way to Athens, Alabama. Bill and his car-less companion, John, lacked much luck finding pickups on the desolate northern Alabama roads, and their ninety-mile trip quickly turned into an all-day affair. Upon finally arriving on campus, they were met with bad news: The football coach, Coach Marvin "Bull" Smith, was not even in town that day.

Ensley High School, ca. 1949

However, Bill didn't return to Pratt City totally dejected. Like most things in Bill's mind, the effort was worth it. As he hitchhiked back the same way he came, Bill did what he did best: He doubled down on his doggedness, decided he wasn't going to be beaten, and made plans to return at the start of the school year.

Suffice it to say, resiliency was never lacking for Bill: When his father ran

In one Ensley High School game played at the Jacksonville, Florida, "Gator Bowl" against Robert E. Lee High School, a star player forgot his knee and thigh pads at home, and Coach McClain quickly called on Bill, standing on the sidelines to hand over his gear to the star player. Later in the game, when the team was down and Bill finally stepped on the field, padless but impassioned, he rushed for the first—and only—first down his team earned all game.

over his bike to teach him a lesson, he picked up that tangled mess of metal and figured out a way to get it fixed. When his father urged him to provide for the family at his barbershop—something Bill didn't want—he refused that path but figured out a way to provide for them anyway. And when his hitchhike expedition up to Athens the first time was met with nothing but disappointment, Bill didn't lose an ounce of gumption.

So when the time came for a return trip at the end of July 1949, Bill scraped together whatever belongings he could muster, quit his job at TCI, and rode with Jim Hodges back up to Athens—a much shorter trip this time.

Bill Thorn, Ensley High School basketball team, ca. 1949

The second time was a charm for Bill, as Coach Smith decided to give Bill a chance and invited him to come to August tryouts. Bill was issued a uniform and given a job in the "Bear's Den"—an on-campus hamburger joint owned by the football program—to make ends meet while he slugged away at the August tryouts. Bill knew that his performance would be critiqued with an eagle eye and would pave the path to one of two possible fates: He would be offered a scholarship and return to pursue his degree, or he would be cut loose, destined to return to the steel mill. He gave his all at practice, giving every ounce of effort and "doing things I didn't think I could do." Bill "got knocked around like crazy, enough to cause anyone to give up," but still didn't relent. Instead, he "thrived" on the aggressiveness.

While Coach Smith was a man who could tower over almost anyone—a broad-shouldered, six-foot, seven-inch, former football All-American from Howard College—he particularly towered over Bill, who weighed in at 130 pounds, the lightest on the entire field.

After the grueling August tryouts, the day came when Coach Smith called Bill over from the field for his verdict. "Peewee," he said, using one of the nicknames he had bestowed upon Bill, "go home and pack."

Tennessee Coal Iron and Railroad Company's furnace, Ensley, Alabama, 1906 (Photo courtesy of the US Library of Congress)

Coach Smith saw something in Bill: Whether it was his determination, pure stubbornness, or unrelenting grit, Bill would never know.

The news overwhelmed Bill, who noted the scholarship opportunity as "the best thing that ever happened to him." *(At the time!)*

"Now, here are the circumstances," Coach Smith continued. "As far as where you can stay, I don't have another room in the athletic dormitory for any more athletes. The only thing I can come up with is that I have an extra room in the back of my house."

Coach Merle E. Smith

At the time, Coach Smith was in his early forties and recently married. However, his wife had no issue with one extra houseguest for the year.

"You'll be eating with us," she told Bill. "And you'll be participating in cleaning up the kitchen."

So only a few months and many bruises later after hearing about the opportunity, Bill was a full-ride student-athlete at Athens College.

The 1949 Athens College football season was filled with ups and downs, but the team finished with a respectable six wins, three losses, and one tie. The team was hopeful that the following season would be even more fruitful, but changing world events extinguished that dream. As the Korean War broke out, football at Athens College was put on hold.

Athens College football players from the Birmingham area. Bill is pictured front row, far right, wearing the #30 jersey.

Most of Bill's teammates were already enlisted in the National Guard, earning an extra thirty dollars per month. Bill wanted to follow their lead, but Coach Smith urged him not to: "You don't want to do that," he told Bill. "You're too young to really know what you're dealing with."

Bill listened, which meant that come the fall of 1950, he was left behind in Alabama as the majority of the team shipped off to Korea. So many boys enlisted that the team failed to fill a practice squad during Bill's second year, taking the opportunity for a fall football season officially off the table.

> *Coach has a way of making self-discipline in all walks of life seem simple. He has little patience for laziness because it just isn't logical to him.*
>
> *—Daniel Salvador, Fayette and Landmark Christian athlete*

With the football program at Athens College dissolving, Bill sought out other prospects to continue his college football career, to no avail. He was invited to play at a junior college in Mississippi, but the money didn't work out; similarly, a scholarship position opened at Florence State—now North Alabama—but the sole position's pay would have to be split between Bill and one other boy, which Bill could not afford.

So Bill returned home in the fall of 1950. He enrolled at Birmingham Southern College, which didn't have a football squad, but Bill found an unexpected opportunity in intramural sports—and he excelled. Although he'd always been an athlete, he proved more skilled at baseball than almost anything he'd ever tried. He had a knack for fielding the ball and ended up as a third baseman due to his strong arm and dependable catching.

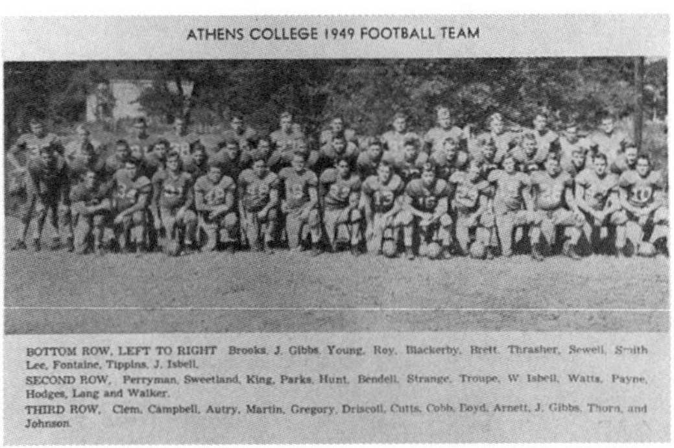

Athens College football team, 1949

And while Bill's baseball skills would eventually earn him a nomination for the Birmingham Southern Athletics Hall of Fame his overall athleticism earned him free tuition, paid by the president of the college himself. This unexpected but much needed financial boost came after Bill joined the Kappa Alpha fraternity, not because Bill was really interested in the camaraderie of the group, but because the boys in the fraternity wanted Bill to join their intramural football, baseball, and basketball teams. As Bill dominated the intramural fields, he was approached by George Stuart, the university's president of more than a decade. Dr. Stuart, a former lawyer and a follower of all of the school's sports (down to the intramural level), knew of Bill and was sympathetic to his story. But most of all, he admired the way Bill could catch a football.

Athens College football game, 1949

With his tuition bill footed by the president, Bill would end up fulfilling his dreams of attending college without burdening anyone with a dime of support.

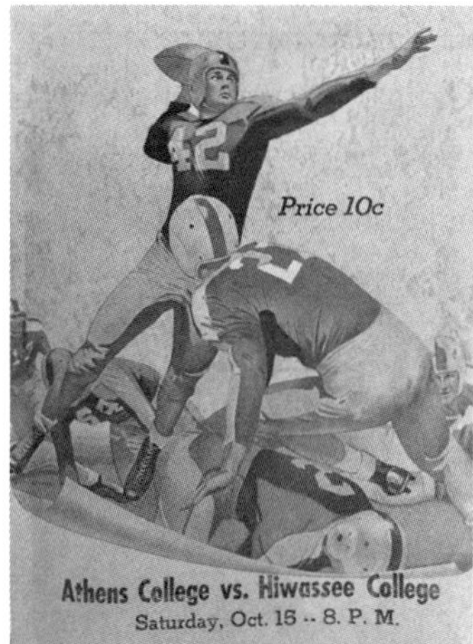

Athens College versus Hiwassee College football program

ATHENS COLLEGE ROSTER

No.	Player	Pos.	Wt.
No.	Player	Pos.	Wt.
10	Smith	FB	180
11	Isbell	G	185
12	King	E	178
13	Brett	FB	175
14	Clem	E	170
15	Young	QB	170
16	Blackerby	HB	160
17	Autry	E	170
18	Logan	HB	191
19	Sewell	HB	185
20	Stephenson	T	194
21	Gibbs	G	175
22	Bendall	HB	175
23	Roy	FB	160
24	Lang	G	172
25	Hunt	T	175
26	Starkey	QB	170
27	Cobb	FB	175
28	Perryman	C	180
29	Walker	G	170
30	Lumpkin	T	178
31	Fontaine	G	170
32	Thrasher	HB	168
33	Strange	E	160
34	Tippins	HB	172
35	Troupe	G	193
36	Johnson	T	209
37	Driskell	FB	193
38	Arnett	T	187
39	Isbell	HB	170
40	Boyd	C	170
41	Payne	T	185
42	Parks	T	215
43	Watts	C	187
44	Cutts	T	205
45	Gregory	T	260
46	Hodges	G	190
47	Gibbs	G	175
48	Smith	C	190
49	F. C. Lee	C	238
50	Martin	FB	183
51	Campbell	HB	146
53	T. Gibbs	C	164
54	Sweetland	G	180
55	Thorn	HB	140

E. M. Smith, Coach

Athens College football roster: Bill is listed bottom right

And as it turned out, it would end up being a side job during his time in college that set the stage for Bill's calling in more ways than one . . .

If you asked Bill at the time about the conversation that set his entire life story in motion—meeting Jim Hodges, who'd been promised a scholarship at Athens College—he probably would have told you it was luck.

But if you'd ask Bill now, at ninety-four, he'd point at that meeting and call it something else: God's handiwork!

Bill couldn't know it then, but that small conversation, that wrinkle in time, that moment where he'd met his coworker at TCI, had changed the entire path of his life forever.

1951 Kappa Alpha intramural football champions (Bill is bottom row, second from right). The KAs ended their season with an impressive 7-1 record and cruised to a decisive victory in the championship KA-ATO game with a score of 14-0

1953 Kappa Alpha intramural football team. (Bill is third from left). The KAs ended their season with a 3-3-1 record, with the "Preachers" team claiming the championship.

FOOTBALL SQUAD

First Row–Tommy Caldwell, Bill Thorn, Terry Carroll, Donald Kendrick, Bob Godwin, Phillip Smith, Ervin Sherer, Johnny Gibson, Bill Carpenter. *Second Row*–Kenneth Burks, Graham Phillips, Roger Wald, Robert Statum, Lucius de Yampert, Brantly King, Donald Brice. *Third Row*–David Blankenhorn, Bobby Wade, Robert Barham, Robert Vandiver, Bill Savage, Vincent Pizzitola, Jack Brown, Lex Rogers. *Fourth Row*–Bill Allen, Don Wilson, Lee Hayley, Ed English, Bill Hart, Harry Mims, Tommy Mitchell, Jimmy Alexander, E. D. Glover.

The Ensley High School football team: Bill is front row, second from left.

Snapshot of the front cover of the Athens College versus Northwest Mississippi football game program, 1949. The original is still in Bill's possession.

Bill as an Athens College athlete

THREE

"YOUR TEAMMATES KEEP YOUR OPPONENTS OFF YOUR NECK"
—THORNISM

THE BIBLE IS FILLED WITH VERSES and scripture that talk about God rejoicing when we find our callings. Romans 12:6 tells us, "We have different gifts, according to the grace given to each of us." And the verses that come after compel us to use those gifts relentlessly, glorifying God as we do.

If your gift is to encourage, the Bible urges, then encourage. If your gift lies in teaching, God smiles down when you teach. If you're a leader, lead fiercely—and do so with diligence. And if your gift is coaching, then by the Lord's will, coach like you were born to do it—because you were.

It's fair to imagine, then, that at the moment Bill stepped into the West Hills YMCA in Birmingham, Alabama, to take his first paid coaching job, there was a joyful noise in the heavens.

The Y had been around almost as long as Birmingham itself: Thirteen years after the city was founded, community leaders established the rec center, complete with religious services, educational classes, library, and—much to Bill's pleasure—a heavy emphasis on athletics.

Bill essentially ran the entire sports program at the Y for two years, where he coached a variety of kids in a variety of sports as a side job while finishing his degree at Birmingham Southern. This gave Bill an incredible opportunity to hone and develop his unique coaching style with the hundreds of kids he came in contact with and find the tools "that worked" to get results.

13-year-old Stars working out—The 13-year-old Western Branch YMCA All-Stars are shown above just before a workout. The team will play Graysville Friday night at Pleasant Grove at 7:30. First row, left to right, are Billy Hunter, pitcher, College Hills; Bill Thorn, coach; Jimmy Liggett, catcher, Pratt City; Jimmy Dempsey, second baseman, Ensley. Back row, left to right, Jerry Johnson, pitcher, Central Park; Frank Walton, first baseman, Wylam; Junior Tomisino, center fielder, West Hills, and Bobby Drennen, third baseman, West End.

Bill alongside his team of thirteen-year-old "All-Stars" before a workout

However, as important as learning how to mentor and teach children, Bill also got his first experience with developing relationships with other young coaches that would last a lifetime. In particular, Bill mentored and worked alongside a young coach named Phil English.

Phil also attended Ensley High School and Birmingham-Southern, albeit a few years behind Bill. "We'd practice and play right next to Legion Field in Birmingham. Phil was just a young man when I knew him, but I taught him what I knew," Bill said. Bill didn't realize it at the time, but the lessons he taught Phil would serve as some of the coaching foundations that Phil used to influence the lives of thousands of boys over the subsequent decades. After coaching at the YMCA, Phil would go on to lead an incredible baseball coaching career—culminating in his induction into the Alabama High School sports Hall of Fame with two stadiums named after him and more than 500 wins in his three-decade baseball coaching career.

A native of Birmingham, Coach Phil English graduated from Ensley High School in 1956. He received his bachelor's degree from Birmingham-Southern College in 1960 and his master's degree in math and science from the University of Alabama in 1966. He returned to his alma mater, Ensley, to begin his coaching career in 1962. His first team compiled a record of 32-0. Eight of his nine starters on that team either turned pro or received a college scholarship. After his three-year coaching stint at Ensley, he took an assistant coaching position at Florida State University for a year. He returned to Birmingham in 1966 to coach at Banks High School for a year. Then Coach English moved over to Huffman High School, where he enjoyed his greatest success over a nineteen-year period. His Huffman team won state championships in 1977 and 1982. His last team at Huffman went 27-7 and finished second in the state. He spent his last six years at Hewitt-Trussville High School. In twenty-eight years of coaching, Coach English saw twelve of his players sign professional contracts and sixty-four of them receive college scholarships to four-year colleges and universities. Three of his Huffman players eventually made it to the major leagues—Britt Burns, Jay Tibbs, and Bill Latham. Between 1971 and 1993, only three of his teams failed to qualify for the state playoffs. His twenty-eight-year career record was 566-217, a winning percentage of .720. Coach English has two high school baseball fields named after him—Huffman, where he built the field out of a swamp, and Hewitt-Trussville, where he built the field out of a cornfield.

City 11-year-old champs—West Hill's 11-year-old YMCA
baseball team took the city title in that age group, and
amassed a 20-2 season's record. Included in the victories
were six no-hitters by Pitcher Charles Weaver. Bottom
row, left to right, Van McCullough, Al Schillaci, Robert
Marshall, Jack Rouss, Howell Raines, David Thompson,
and Coach Bill Thorn. Second row, Clanton Walton,
James Hernandez, Bob Pass, Steve Perry, Larry Sinque-
field, and Bill Braswell. Top row, Coach Phil English,
Ronald Burkett, Weaver, Tom Rogers, and Pat Rogers.

Bill, Phil English, and Clanton Walton as part of the eleven-year-old championship baseball team

Biography courtesy of the
Alabama Baseball Coaches Association Hall of Fame

The YMCA coaching role also introduced Bill to something that he would become very accustomed to: coaching winning teams. One of his very first teams as head coach, the West Hills eleven-year-old boys' baseball team, proudly took the city title and ended the season with an incredible 20-2 record. However, this baseball team would mean more to Bill than almost any other team he ever coached because this particular team was the reason Bill met his future wife and lifelong partner.

Maxie Baughan, photo courtesy of The New York Times

When Bill Thorn moved back to Birmingham to attend Birmingham-Southern, he received some scholarship money for tuition, but he still needed to pay the bills to live. Bill took on three different jobs at the same time: youth counselor at Bessemer Methodist Church, salesclerk at Dixie Sporting Goods (a job Coach Smith had arranged before Bill left Athens College), and coach at the West Hills YMCA. The Youth Counselor job required Bill to travel to Bessemer, Alabama, each Sunday. Bill would travel to Bessemer and attend church with a local family (Maxie Baughan's). After church, he would stay at the Baughans' house for lunch, take a nap, and then hang out with Maxie until it was time to bring Maxie to the youth group he was working at. Bill would mentor young Maxie Baughan until Bill was married and left for Atlanta. Maxie Baughan would go on to be a standout athlete at Bessemer High School, an All-American college football player at Georgia Tech (playing for the legendary coach Bobby Dodd), and a second-round draft pick by the Philadelphia Eagles in 1960. During his pro-football career, Maxie Baughan was a nine-time Pro Bowl selection. Maxie was later inducted into the College Football Hall of Fame, Philadelphia Eagles Hall of Fame, Georgia Tech Hall of Fame, State of Georgia and the State of Alabama Halls of Fame, and the Gator Bowl Hall of Fame. While Bill was coaching at Headland High School and Maxie was playing at Georgia Tech, Maxie would come by to watch the track meets and talk to his youth counselor and coach, Bill Thorn. After Maxie's playing days ended in 1971, he returned to Georgia Tech as a coach and resumed his visits with Coach Thorn until he moved on to a successful twenty-year career coaching NFL and college football. One Headland athlete told us while interviewing him for this book,

> *"Here we are at a track meet, and standing by the high jump pit is Maxie Baughan, the captain of the Georgia Tech football team! We all knew who he was, and we couldn't believe it when he wanted to talk to Coach Thorn."*

Eleven-year-old Clanton Walton was a standout player for Bill. During one game, however, Bill's eyes drifted away from Clanton's play on the diamond to a breathtaking spectator in the stands who just happened to be Clanton's older sister, Patty. Patty was at home on summer break after her freshman year at the University of Chattanooga, where she was studying for a two-year secretarial degree. "She was a beautiful girl, although she downplays that," Bill recollected, and he immediately began to devise a clever way to ask her out.

Patty Walton

So he did what any young man does when he wants to ask a pretty girl on a date—he persuaded somebody else to ask her out for him.

"He asked my mother's best friend, Mrs. Perry, if I wanted to come watch him play fast-pitch softball," Patty recalled.

This wasn't just any ordinary game Bill was inviting his future wife to: It was the 1953 Southeastern Regional Softball World Championships qualifier in Clearwater, Florida. Bill was thrilled Patty agreed to come watch him play; however, it wasn't exactly "happily ever after" immediately . . .

1953 Southeastern Softball Tournament program

As Patty explained, she started smoking a cigarette on the way down to Clearwater. This did not impress Bill at all and prompted a very clear ultimatum. Patty recalled Bill's exact words: "If I ever see you with a cigarette in your mouth again, I'll never speak to you again . . . That is the ugliest thing I've ever seen." Patty gave up the habit immediately. Fortunately, she "didn't like them much anyway."

Despite this initial romantic hiccup, Patty and Bill "went steady" that summer, before Patty returned to school and Bill enrolled in his senior year at Birmingham-Southern. Although Patty was two hours away, Patty's mother, Mary, was close by, and Bill would visit often.

Patty with her mother, Mary, on Bill and Patty's wedding day, 1954

Mary Walton was brilliant and well educated—a French major who was forced to drop out of her last year of college when the Depression hit. Even without a formal degree, she frequently helped Bill with his own collegiate coursework, ensuring he made the requisite grades needed to graduate on time.

As time passed, Bill and Patty saw each other when time allowed, and Patty's mother began to question her daughter about the future of the relationship.

"Do you like Bill?" she asked her daughter one day, to which Patty responded that she did.

"Would you think about marrying anybody else?" she asked. "Well," Patty recalled saying, "I don't *know* anybody else."

That settled it.

When Patty came home for Christmas, Patty's mother gave Bill her grandmother's diamond ring. Her mother planned a wedding for the following June, almost one year to the day that Bill first saw Patty in the baseball stands. But just because she was planning the wedding didn't mean that Mary saw the couple together forever. Knowing Bill's strong will, she told Patty's father, "I don't think this marriage is going to last."

Even with maternal doubts looming, on June 11, 1954, in the Church of the Advent in Birmingham, Alabama, Bill and Patty wed. However, that wasn't Bill's only commitment that day. Prior to the wedding, Bill coached at the YMCA track championships. When asked later if she was upset that their wedding plans revolved around Bill's coaching schedule, Patty simply stated, "No. That's just what Bill did, and we got married afterward!"

Bill and Patty's wedding

Bill and Patty wouldn't remain in Birmingham long. One week before marrying Patty, Bill officially graduated with his bachelor of arts degree in physical education from Birmingham Southern. Deciding to continue his pursuit of higher education, Bill and Patty packed up what belongings they had and moved to Atlanta for Bill to attend seminary at Emory University. To earn an income while Bill was in school, Patty found a job at Life of Georgia Insurance using a Dictaphone for note-taking, while Bill found an array of odd jobs, such as refereeing, to pay the bills.

> *His love for God, Mrs. Patty, and his family are what people remember most about him. Mrs. Patty is always by his side and has the most infectious, beautiful smile.*
>
> *—Lindy Long Jones, Landmark Christian and US Air Force Academy athlete*

Emory didn't turn out the way Bill had anticipated, though. Up until this point, Bill was acquainted with religion but didn't have a relationship with the Lord. He wasn't saved. He wasn't enthusiastic about attending,

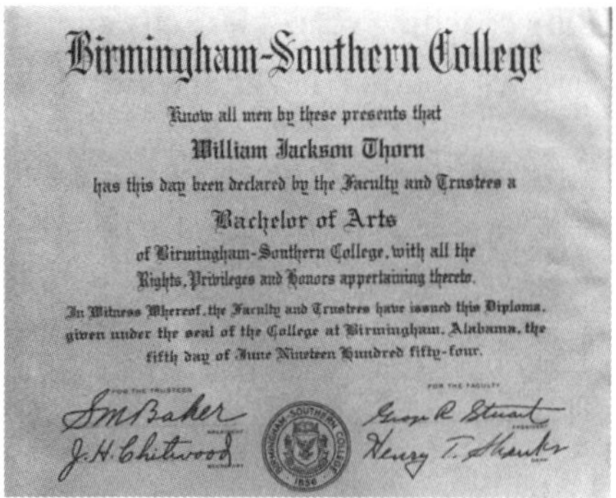

Birmingham-Southern College

Know all men by these presents that
William Jackson Thorn
has this day been declared by the Faculty and Trustees a
Bachelor of Arts
of Birmingham-Southern College, with all the
Rights, Privileges and Honors appertaining thereto.

In Witness Whereof, the Faculty and Trustees have issued this Diploma,
given under the seal of the College at Birmingham, Alabama, the
fifth day of June Nineteen Hundred fifty-four.

Bill's degree from Birmingham-Southern

and he'd largely gone ahead with the seminary plan at the behest of his father's sister, Aunt Margie, who wanted him to become a Methodist minister.

Bill stuck it out for one semester—although he knew the vocation wasn't for him on the first day of classes. "They were just telling jokes," he said. "There was a class about 'The Art of Preaching,' where they practiced every move to make with your hands, every gesture, every best joke. Golly, it was highly organized. I thought, 'If that's all we're doing, I'm out of here.' I didn't think that's what the Lord's work was . . . to try to fake it . . . so I was done with that."

Bill's yearbook photo from Emory University, 1955

Howard Dial, Bill's longtime reverend and friend, reflected on what Bill told him about those first few days attending seminary at Emory: "Bill had a bit of a Methodist background," he said. "But he wasn't a Christian—not in that mindset yet anyway. What he discovered at Emory was not the Methodists he grew up with—the ones from his mother's generation."

Howard wasn't in Bill's life at the time he attended Emory, but he knows this about Bill: He's principled. And likely, watching the theatrics of these classes and watching fellow attendees question the authority of the Bible didn't sit well with Bill—even as a non-Christian.

Bill returning a punt while playing intramural tackle football at Emory University.

The focus on theatrics over theology drove Bill away and straight back into the calling that he'd loved so much at the YMCA in Birmingham: coaching.

Bill, far right, third row, as an assistant coach for the GMA football team

A listing for an opening at Georgia Military Academy (or GMA, later to be renamed Woodward Academy) provided Bill the opportunity to serve as the runningback and physical development coach for the football team, while teaching eighth-graders, as he put it, "everything in science and social studies that existed." He also took on the job of coaching varsity basketball "since no one else wanted it," even though he had no idea how to coach the sport—despite being a skilled point guard in his younger days. Learning from experienced coaches around the Atlanta area, Bill focused on conditioning the players as his top priority while learning how to teach winning basketball from a coach's perspective.

While he thrived in leading the kids through exercises, drill work, and calisthenics, he wasn't too fond of the disciplinary duties of the role, including nightly rounds to ensure the boys were in their beds. "The older they were, the more problems there were," he claimed. The student body was primarily comprised of boys sent away by their parents, who Patty—also having shared the dormitory halls with the high schoolers—described as "mischievous."

Fran Tarkenton

Francis Tarkenton was a standout athlete in football, basketball, and baseball at Athens High School in Athens, Georgia. It was during Fran's senior year that he and Coach Thorn ran into each other—not just once, but twice. In 1956, after leading the Athens High football team to an undefeated season and state championship as quarterback, Fran's senior year at guard on the basketball team resulted in an 11-2 record, with two of those eleven wins coming against Coach Thorn's GMA basketball squad. Coach Thorn said, "There was this young fellow up there in Athens that was such a great leader on the court. The first time we played Athens, I thought we would have won that game, but he really came to play, and we lost by about four points. The second time we played Athens, they were ready for us and got us good. I believe that guard was this kid named Francis Tarkenton—you ever hear of him?" Suffice it to say, a lot of people have "heard" of Fran Tarkenton—the All-SEC quarterback at the University of Georgia, an NFL quarterback for eighteen years, and a Pro Football Hall of Fame, College Football Hall of Fame, and Georgia Sports Hall of Fame inductee.

Bill and Patty lived in a two-bedroom suite in a student dormitory called Rugby Hall, enjoying free room and board in addition to an extra 120 dollars per month Bill received for his pay as a dormitory parent for the live-in students. The noise and constant commotion from the students wasn't an ideal first home for the couple, but the free meals at the dining hall and inexpensive living arrangements made the less-than-ideal conditions worth it.

It was during their second year living on campus that Bill and Patty welcomed an additional source of noise to the hallways: their first baby. As Bill recalled, "My first thought when I found out we were pregnant was, 'How do we pay for this?'" In fact, Bill was so concerned about the financials of the pregnancy that at the first obstetrics appointment, Bill struck a deal with the physician for the birth, thereby allowing Bill to save up for the incoming hospital bill. However, Bill forgot one critical thing in preparing for the baby's arrival—memorizing the directions to the hospital.

Rugby Hall

As Patty recollected, finding themselves lost at 11:00 p.m. with a baby arriving any moment, Bill "asked a drunk man on the street for directions to the hospital, and we almost ran out of gas on the way."

Bill as an instructor at GMA

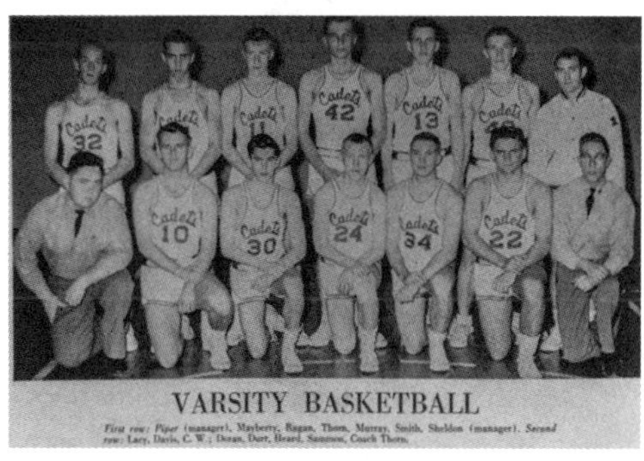

GMA basketball team, ca. 1957

With just twenty minutes to spare, Bill and Patty arrived in their Oldsmobile at Old Piedmont Hospital on June 8, 1956, and welcomed a daughter, Patricia Lynn Thorn, or "Lynn" for short, into the world. Lynn would turn out to be blond like her daddy, and equally prudent, smart, and stubborn. "We'd tell her not to jump on the bed, but she wouldn't listen until she fell and got a black eye," said Patty.

Capt. Thorn GMA yearbook photo, ca. 1956

Backfield Coach Thorn

Bill holding baby Lynn

The Thorn Family Christmas card, 1957

Bill and Patty's second child, Cheryl, would arrive in May two years later. With now four mouths in total to feed, Bill started looking for ways to better fund and house his growing family. But as Bill looked for other opportunities, it turned out someone was looking for him. That someone was Coach Nolan Lang.

The GMA Coaching Years Recap:
4 years as Head Basketball Coach
4 years as Assistant Football Coach

Thorn family circa 1958

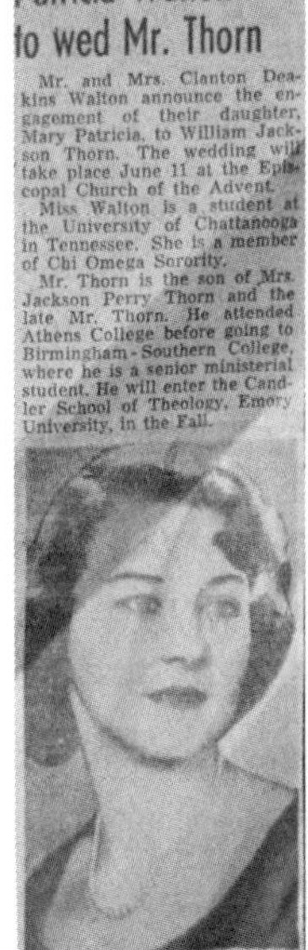

Patricia Walton to wed Mr. Thorn

Mr. and Mrs. Clanton Deakins Walton announce the engagement of their daughter, Mary Patricia, to William Jackson Thorn. The wedding will take place June 11 at the Episcopal Church of the Advent.

Miss Walton is a student at the University of Chattanooga in Tennessee. She is a member of Chi Omega Sorority.

Mr. Thorn is the son of Mrs. Jackson Perry Thorn and the late Mr. Thorn. He attended Athens College before going to Birmingham-Southern College, where he is a senior ministerial student. He will enter the Candler School of Theology, Emory University, in the Fall.

Miss Mary Patricia Walton

Bill and Patty's wedding announcement in the local newspaper

Bill's youth football squad at the Y

"I ain't never been nothin' but a winner."
—Paul "Bear" Bryant . . . also, Bill Thorn

I love this quote by Bear Bryant. I think it was accurate in describing the great Crimson Tide coach. I also think it is accurate in describing Coach Bill Thorn. When you examine his life, athletic career, coaching career, and family, it is evident. Bill Thorn is a winner, and throughout his life, he has influenced thousands of others to be winners as well.

In the 1950s, amateur sports were huge in the Birmingham area. It was a release for hardworking men after a long day. In a day and time in Alabama when most people didn't have a lot of money to afford luxuries such as TVs, fancy restaurants, movies, or vacations, amateur sports provided an outlet. It was a way to "let off steam," have fun competing, and enjoy friendships with your teammates.

Most of the time, teams were made up of men who worked together or went to church together. It wasn't uncommon for a business or factory to hire a man to work for them because he would be a great addition to the basketball or softball team. It was also a great way for a church to evangelize and grow. The church's main mission is to spread the gospel and minister to its members. If a new member just happens to be a great shortstop or outfielder, even better!

Birmingham-Southern baseball team, date unknown

Bill got involved in the amateur sports scene because of the relationship that he had with two men. One was his high school Basketball and Baseball Coach at Ensley High School, Claude McClain. Coach McClain took an active role in the community and, in addition to his duties at Ensley, he was very involved in local amateur sports as a coach, player, and official. He was also very involved in organizing leagues and putting teams together. The other was a close friend named Harold Myhand. The two had met at Birmingham-Southern College and became friends. They were both involved in the school's intramural program, and they were both highly competitive. Harold attended West End Church and played on their basketball and softball teams. They played against high-level competition, often against nonchurch teams. Harold recruited Bill to join their group, and he fit right in. Coach Thorn was such a talented player and would catch the eyes of other teams and coaches in the area, who would recruit him to come and play for them for the season or for weekend tournaments. Being the ultimate competitor, he was always willing and up for the challenge.

A young Bill Thorn in his twenties dominated the hardwoods and diamonds across central Alabama. He was somewhat of a local legend as he competed in contests in towns like Bessemer, Irondale, Pelham, Jasper, Fayette, Tuscaloosa, and Gadsden.

His teams often won city, league, and state championships, and often competed on the national level. His 1953 softball team, Thomas Sporting Goods from Bessemer, Alabama, defeated the nationally renowned Clearwater Bombers in the first round of the national, regional tournament. Unfortunately, the Bombers came back from the losers' bracket and defeated the group from Bessemer in the championship to advance to the World Series. Even though they lost in the championship round, they won the respect of the Bombers and the softball world.

Trophy for champs—Members of the Thomas Sporting Goods softball team lined up for the cameramen as they were given their trophy for the Jefferson County Metropolitan softball championship.

Standing, left to right, Tommy Graham, Morris Bunn, James Mann, Coach Nash Carmichael, Buck House, Cecil Martin, Sgt. A. E. O'Brien, sponsor Bill Thomas, Manager Jason Dean, L. C. Barrow, representative of the Coca-Cola Co., which presented the trophy, and Metropolitan Commissioner King Sparks. Kneeling, Bill Thorn, Buddy Hall, Dean Taylor, Cotton Anderton and Jack Griffin. In front, Batboy Butch Taylor. Catcher Rabbit Gray was not present.

Bill, as a member of the Thomas Sporting Goods softball team, receiving the championship trophy

Bobby Marlowe and Harry Gilmer were two of Bill Thorn's Alabama heroes. Those two men were Crimson Tide stars of the 1940s and 1950s who cast a long shadow over the state. Bill Thorn cast a long shadow himself: He was an outstanding player and teammate and was well known and respected by his fellow competitors, as evidenced by the many honors and awards that were bestowed upon him over the *years. Because of his success, the Central Alabama Amateur Softball Hall of Fame honored Bill Thorn with induction in 1997.*

—Wayne Brantley, fellow Coach and Instructor with Coach Thorn at Landmark Christian School

FOUR

"WHEN IT'S TOO TOUGH FOR THEM, IT'S JUST RIGHT FOR US" —THORNISM

COACH NOLAN LANG WAS A LEGEND. As recounted by the Waycross-Ware County Sports Hall of Fame, at the young age of sixteen, he earned a spot as a starting defensive back and fullback for the Alabama Polytechnic University (now Auburn University) and was the youngest player on the team for the two years he played there. Although his collegiate football days were interrupted by his service in the US Army during World War II, he continued to excel athletically as a sprinter, shot-put thrower, and member of the Fort Benning Doughboys football team as they claimed the Army's national championship. When he completed his service time, Lang returned to college athletics as the fullback for Coach Bud Wilkerson at the University of Oklahoma and helped lead the team to the 1950 Sugar Bowl title.

Coach Nolan Lang, courtesy of the Waycross-Ware County Sports Hall of Fame

Following graduation, Lang took a job as the Football Coach at Headland High School in East Point, Georgia. Still young himself, he became known for his amenable nature and friendliness toward the players.

PREP BEAT

BILL THORN LEAVES GMA TO COACH HEADLAND BACKS

By GENE ASHER

Bill Thorn, assistant coach at GMA the past three years, has joined with Headland staff as backfield coach. He also will assist with either basketball or baseball. . . . You

into the No. 1 quarterback assignment at Dudley Hughes.

• • •

OF HALFBACK Jimmy Burson (LaGrange, South All-Star), Auburn freshman coach Erskine

Press release announcing Bill's new job at Headland High School

Coach Lang knew potential when he saw it, and what he saw in Bill was the making of another legend. Coach Lang recruited Bill to join Headland's football coaching staff, which Bill did in 1959 at the rate of 317 dollars per month. Working under Coach Lang for two years, Bill continued to hone his football tactics and coaching skills, eventually earning the Head Coach position at Headland when Coach Lang moved to a neighboring school.

Proud to lead the Headland Highlanders, Bill set out to truly establish himself as a coach and leader. Headland was where Bill, inarguably, cut his teeth at building his no-nonsense, gritty, run-like-you-mean-it reputation in a more public and visible setting.

COACH BILL THORN
Varsity Football, Track

COACH CHARLIE BROWN
Varsity Football, Wrestling

COACH JACK SHORT
B-Team Football, Soccer

COACH OTIS MABRY
8th Grade Football; B-Team and 8th Grade Basketball

Headland High School Coaches, 1961

Sure, at GMA, he'd implemented a lot of the same tough coaching strategies that built good character, instilled mental toughness, and pushed players to their limits. But at Headland, where Bill was the Head Football

Form A-1000 Rev. 1959

DUPLICATE

CONTRACT OF EMPLOYMENT

STATE OF GEORGIA
COUNTY OF

This Agreement, made and executed this the 25th day of AUGUST, 1959, between the FULTON COUNTY BOARD OF EDUCATION (Name of Employing Body) of FULTON County, Georgia of the first part (hereinafter called the employer,) and WILLIAM J. THORN, 1081 BEN HILL RD., EAST POINT, GA. (P. O. Address), of the second part (hereinafter called teacher):

WITNESSETH: That in compliance with Georgia Code Annotated, Section 32-604 and pursuant to the terms, conditions, and agreements hereinafter expressed, which are mutually acknowledged to be of good and sufficient consideration therefor, the employer has employed the teacher, and the teacher has accepted employment, as a member of the teaching staff of the public school system of FULTON County, Georgia, for the scholastic year commencing with the first of the month following entrance into service after its formal opening in 1959 and closing in 1960, at a salary of $317.00 per month, payable monthly for 12 months, subject to adjustment according to Georgia Code Annotated, Sections 32-603 to 32-608 inclusive included in the "MINIMUM FOUNDATION PROGRAM," applicable to the classification and type of service to which the teacher has been assigned, without obligation by the employer to make up any deficit beyond such sum as shall become uniformly applicable to all teachers of the same group, classification, type and length of service, as determined by any law or laws now or hereafter in operation regulating the financing of public school systems within said County, and/or Independent school district under the local jurisdiction whereof the school affected hereby may be administered.

The teacher agrees to observe such curriculum and standards and obey such reasonable rules and regulations as may from time to time be put in force by appropriate lawful action of the employer, in compliance with the uniform practices prescribed by authority of the State Board of Education of the State of Georgia.

It is understood that the teacher is assigned to the duty of teaching at HEADLAND HIGH SCHOOL (Name of School) located at EAST POINT, GEORGIA (City, Town or Center), in said County, but the employer reserves the right to effect a transfer at any time to any school under the jurisdiction of the employer. This CONTRACT OF EMPLOYMENT may be terminated at any time upon two weeks' notice in writing by either party communicated to the other, for lawful cause. The teacher agrees, furthermore, to execute and subscribe to such oath or affirmation of allegiance to the Government and Constitution respectively, of the United States and of the State of Georgia as may be required by law, and to execute a written questionnaire concerning his or her personal history, qualification, and loyalty.

It is also agreed that in the event of the termination hereof for any reason prior to the completion of the aforesaid scholastic year, the amount payable hereunder shall represent the monthly rate of salary for the number of months during which such employment has continued and services have been rendered.

The terms and conditions of this Contract are made expressly subject to the provisions of the Constitution and laws of the State of Georgia relating to public education and the appropriations therefor. Furthermore, it is mutually understood and agreed that in the event any school in said County to which the employee is assigned to teach under this Contract is closed by an Executive Order of the Govennor of Georgia then this Contract shall immediately terminate and there shall be no liability whatever after the date of such closing against the FULTON County Board of Education under the provisions of this Contract. However, the employee named in this Contract shall be entitled to all the benefits provided by the State of Georgia in House Bill No. 374 passed at the 1959 Session of the General Assembly of Georgia which was signed by the Governor on March 17, 1959, and is now Act. No. 382. (Ga. Laws 1959, p. 350.)

Salary payable hereunder shall be deemed earned during the active school year but is payable in 12 monthly installments throughout fiscal year.

IN WITNESS WHEREOF, The parties hereto have hereunto executed this CONTRACT OF EMPLOYMENT, by setting their hands and seals in duplicate, the day and year first above written.

FULTON COUNTY Board of Education
City or County

FULTON County, Georgia

(SEAL)

BY: Paul D. West
Superintendent of Schools
Employer, Party of the First Part

William J. Thorn (SEAL)
Employer, Party of the Second Part

Bill's original employment contract with Fulton County Schools, 1959

Bill teaching at Headland High School, 1959

Lang Relinquishes Helm at Headland

Thorn Takes Over As Head Grid Coach

NOLAN LANG
. . . Thorn His Successor

By PAUL ATKINSON

Nolan Lang has resigned as head football coach at Headland High School and will be succeeded by Bill Thorn.

Lang tendered his resignation in a surprise move Friday; and, immediately, Thorn was elevated to the position.

"It's with deep regret that we accept Mr. Lang's resignation as football coach," said Headland principal Paul Lewis. "But it was something he decided he wanted to do; he will stay on and teach social studies."

"This was the toughest decision of my life," said Lang.

"I owe everything I've ever had to football; it's been tremendously good to me—I've made many friends through it.

"But I just feel that this is the best time to step out of the game. It hurt to quit, believe me."

Lang, 33, had been the only football coach Headland has had in its four years of existence. After a rugged indoctrination period as a new school, the Highlanders have come on quickly in the last two seasons to win all but three games in 20 decisions.

The husky Lang, who was a starting tailback for Auburn at the age of 16 and later was No. 2 fullback behind All-American Leon Heath at Oklahoma, is credited with laying a solid foundation for years to come at Headland. "Our eighth-grade program is one of the best," said Lang in explanation.

Lang got his coaching start at

man with a run-plating double past first base. Dave Nicholson's high fly hit inside the right foul line for a two-run triple, and he came home, too, when Wallace's relay hit the grandstand back of third base.

Lead-off singles by Pete Ward and Roger McCardall and a fielder's choice on Daniel's chopper to the mound cost Rowe a run in the second inning of the nightcap.

Tech Cagers Add Missouri

Georgia Tech, already tackling one of the toughest grid schedules in the country, Friday announced a stiffened 1961-62 cage schedule including four new highly ranked opponents.

Athletic Director Bobby Dodd

olina State, South Carolina and Duke are the 1960-61 opponents dropped to make room for the new slate.

Local press release announcing Nolan Lang's resignation and Bill's promotion to Head Coach

and Track Coach, it was much more noticeable—to parents, the school staff, opposing teams, and especially to the players.

When Bill eventually took the helm as Head Coach, word quickly spread. As one player put it, "There was a new sheriff in town"—a sheriff who certainly didn't care about being a "friend," as he set the tone for a much different locker room than his predecessor.

Bill didn't experience success immediately. In 1961, his first year as head football coach, the team went 4-6, winning their first three games before crumbling. Though many factors contributed to the team's faltering—like Bill's aggressive play calling and strategy of going for first downs rather than punting the ball—none stood out more than the team's lack of conditioning.

To fix this glaring Achilles' heel, Bill quickly implemented a new and demanding training and conditioning regimen, modeled after the most aggressive college programs. Moving forward, all football players would be required to run track, complete a rigorous summer conditioning program, and participate in a new year-round weight-lifting schedule. Additionally, Bill began to craft his first set of motivational and inspirational slogans to get his players in the correct mindset. These phrases, poems, slogans, and quotes would eventually come to be known as "Thornisms," or bits of Bill Thorn wisdom shared with his athletes as motivation to excel and achieve. For many athletes, these "Thornisms" became quick reminders to keep fighting when times got tough and became so memorable they continued to serve the players long after their sporting days were over. After all, "Quitters never win, and winners never quit." At Headland in particular, Bill mounted a poem by Walter Wintle in the locker room and required the athletes to recite it before every game. When shortened, Bill would often recite the critical phrase, "If you think you are beaten, you are," to get the team back in the right mindset. Although the original version of the poem remains largely unknown and debated, the following is the version used by Coach Thorn and the version the Headland players came to memorize:

Headland High School track team, 1963

"It's All in a State of Mind," Walter D. Wintle, 1905

If you think you are beaten, you are.
If you think you dare not, you won't.
If you like to win, but you think you can't,
It's almost a cinch you won't.

If you think you'll lose, you've lost.
For out in the world, you find.
Success begins with a fellow's will.
It's all in the state of mind.

Full many a game is lost.
Ere ever a play is run.
And many a coward fail.
Ere ever his work's begun.

Think big and your deeds will grow.
Think small and you'll fall behind.
Think you can and you will;
It's all in the state of mind.

If you think you're outclassed, you are.
You've got to think high to rise.
You've got to be sure of yourself before
You can ever win a prize.

Life's battles don't always go
To the stronger or faster man.
But sooner or later, the man who wins,
Is the fellow who thinks he can.

The Headland High School football players presented Coach Thorn with a plaque of the Walter Wintle poem at the team's 2014 reunion. The poem had such an effect on the players that most can recite it to this day, and many point to the poem as a source of strength and motivation throughout their lives.

For Bill, his coaching philosophy could largely be summed up in that poem. But it also could be summed up as a person's struggle to get to heaven. It's a narrow gate and a tougher road, and not everyone wants to walk it. But the narrow gate is the only path, and in Bill's mind, a narrow gate in football conditioning, as in life, was the only path to success.

After all, as Bill said, "Track and football are a lot alike. As long as you understand that heavy breathing and sweating won't kill you, you'll do just fine."

In addition to requiring the football players to participate in track, Bill also started soccer at Headland with the intention of using it as an offseason conditioning sport for his football boys. "I didn't even think about the fact that they would stick with it," he recounted years later. Bill didn't know much about coaching soccer skills, which was reflected in the team's games: "We almost destroyed Westminster. They were all complaining that our kids would miss the ball and kick their shins instead. They [Westminster players] were all limping all over the place. And not only that, we didn't have uniforms. We just wore football jerseys." Despite a lack of understanding of the nuances of soccer, Coach Thorn was successful in his first season and ended with a not-too-shabby record of 3-4-1.

Headland High School soccer team wearing football jerseys, ca. 1962

Headland was also the place where Bill began to truly refine and implement his unique version of physical conditioning, which he simply called "The Program." According to Bill, and many of the athletes who followed "The Program," the results

Entrance of Hard Labor Creek State Park

spoke for themselves: If you stuck to "The Program," you'd be a success; if you didn't, you were on your own. In a sense, Bill's version of "The Program" put a mirror up to each athlete, illuminating who each was as a young adult, as well as who they could be. For those who took on the challenge to improve, the rewards were immeasurable.

Coach Thorn also started the wrestling program at Headland High School and hired the school's first Wrestling Coach, Charlie Brown.

Along with weightlifting, track, soccer, and "The Program," Coach Thorn overhauled the school's football summer camp. Modeled after Bear Bryant's Texas A&M football camp, Coach Thorn would gather the team at the appropriately named Hard Labor Creek State Park for an ultimate test of physical and mental endurance. Featuring 5:00 a.m. wake-ups and two-a-day practices in the sweltering Georgia heat with few-and-far-between water breaks (during this time, water was not considered necessary during training), Coach Thorn's football camp truly pushed all players to their physical and mental limits.

Interior of a Hard Labor Creek State park cabin, where the football players stayed during camp

Mike Bell, a former Headland player, recalled his first day of 1962 camp vividly: "Camp started on a Sunday. On the bus ride down, we thought, 'Coach won't make us do anything on a Sunday!' We got to camp, popped popcorn, drank sodas . . . Then, Coach called us to the field to start running, full stomachs and all. The field was ringed by tall trees, so the humidity just stayed there." Suffice it to say, you can imagine what happened to the popcorn and sodas.

Not knowing much about the dangers of heat exhaustion and dehydration, players were given dextrose for their dry mouths. In later years, Bill allowed players to drink from a garden hose—but like everything else under Bill's leadership, it was regulated.

Headland players during Bull in the Ring

Bill also gave players the opportunity to prove themselves through tough drills such as "Bull in the Ring." Bill recalled one particular boy, Ken Lewis, who was "gifted in hitting you aggressively, but looked the opposite." Players were assigned a number that would be called out at random by Bill to "meet" in the middle of a circle and knock one another out of the ring. This drill gave each boy a platform to step up and demonstrate his strength and aggressiveness. "Ken's mother had washed his jersey and brought it to him at the fence at school one day," Bill remembered. "The kids kind of made fun . . . but [the Bull in the Ring] is how he gained respect . . . And that toughness earned him an appointment to play football at the Military Academy at West Point." (Ken wasn't alone in this path; this toughness would become a hallmark of a Bill Thorn–coached athlete and the beginning of a sixty-year string of Military Academy athletes.) However, not all the boys were so willing to put in the hard labor required at Hard Labor Creek. One boy—a senior offensive center who was new to the team—infamously disappeared. The road into camp was long and dusty—maybe fifteen miles or so—but that didn't deter the runaway. On the drive in, the young boy was looking back the whole way, plotting his escape. He left in the middle of the night for a long walk back to town, and the team never saw him again—at camp, school, or elsewhere!

Headland High School coaching staff

Following their popcorn-fueled opening workout, camp conditions in 1962 continued to prove particularly brutal. One day, blinding rain flooded the fields, thunder abounded, and lightning struck in the distance. "I guess it's raining too hard for us to practice today," Bill remarked—a rarity for anyone who knew his willingness to train, rain or shine. Often, he'd tell his players, "Rain or mud, sweat or blood, a lone ranger is going to ride." In other words, it didn't matter what the weather was like—they were practicing. The boys, relieved, gathered their belongings for an afternoon off. Then, as if Bill had a direct line to talk to God, the clouds parted, the rain subsided, and the thunder quieted. The skies cleared, just as Bill changed his tune and ordered the boys to don their uniforms and get to work.

Bill commented, "Players might've thought, 'It's my way or the highway.' You might say that, but that's not how I looked at it. I believe it's the right way, and I'm standing for right."

However, not all the teenage minds under his steadfast leadership agreed. That night in the cabins, the boys were ready to mutiny. The thick, muggy, poststorm air hung heavy, and mud clogged their cleats from hours of slogging in the fields. Many shared the same sentiment: The grind wasn't worth it. They'd devoted their lives to this sport and to this man. They couldn't complain at home, as almost every set of parents had bought into the system too. They couldn't complain at practice or break the rules, or they'd be shown the way out. It was the first time some had been challenged to their core, and many were struggling to reconcile whether or not they could handle the demands placed upon them. Many also questioned being a Headland Highlander, in particular. They played the Tigers, Bears, and other ostensibly fierce and obviously intimidating opponents. *What was so special about a Highlander?*

Cocaptains John Till and Jimmy Jordan on the field during the 1962 season

Bill Curry as a College Park High School football player, ca. 1959

Bill Curry first ran into Coach Bill Thorn at GMA in basketball and then Headland High School in football. Although Curry would go on to become a starting center for the legendary Coach Bobby Dodd at Georgia Tech ('62-'64) followed by 10 seasons in the NFL as a player and Super Bowl champion, his playing days against Bill Thorn–coached teams were less than spectacular.

Following his NFL playing career, Bill Curry was the Head Football Coach at Georgia Tech (1980-1986), the University of Alabama (1987-1989), the University of Kentucky (1990-1996), and Georgia State University (2008-2012). During his coaching days, he would visit Coach Thorn at Coach's Tire Shop in College Park, and Coach Thorn would visit Coach Curry during team visits to the University of Alabama. Bill Curry said the following about Coach Thorn:

"I first met Coach Thorn when I was an athlete at College Park High School in the late '50s. First, we competed with Woodward Academy (then Georgia Military Academy) in basketball and later against Headland High School in football. He went out of his way to speak and encourage us when we went to Woodward, even though we were the opponents. My experience with his team at Headland was not as pleasant. I was an overrated linebacker, and they wore me out, all fair and square! Coach Thorn and his associates had them ready and taught me a great lesson in humility. Believe it or not, some of his guys still tease me about it, but Bill never has."

The team gathered in an old shed to hash out their next plans: quit, mutiny, or stick with Coach Thorn. Tensions were high and emotions were strong. One boy, John Till, felt the urge to step up and "settle everybody down." Playing guard at a lean 145 pounds (although the football roster padded his weight to read 160), Till was entering his senior year and didn't want to see the team fall apart. Through tears, he mustered every ounce of courage he had and delivered an impactful speech to remind everyone that they weren't beaten, and to stay the course. "Let's get it together, boys," Till said. "It's time to get tough. Coach Thorn loves us, and this is the way he demonstrates his love. You gotta hang in there . . . He's trying to make us into a good team." This speech, along with words from several other players, including Jimmy Jordan and Mickey King, quelled the mutiny. No one quit.

The Bible talks about perseverance. I don't know that I would have been able to understand that back then. Most of the games in our junior and senior years that were successful, we won in the third and fourth quarters. It wasn't just because of conditioning—it was perseverance. But there was an inner quality that Coach exemplified for us and taught us. It's perseverance, not quitting.

—Brian Anderson, Headland High School athlete

Our team was so small that in both home and away programs, Coach Thorn wouldn't let them print our size or weight. We had our number, our position, our name, and our class—that was it. Nobody ever told anybody how small we really were.

One of our offensive guards, Freddie Reeves, was a senior. He was five feet eight and weighed 148 pounds. And that was because he had his helmet, his cleats, and his pads on when they took his height and weight.

—Greg Ward, Headland High School football and track athlete

This meeting in the shed became a memorable life event for the Headland players, with many still able to vividly recall the details of the momentous gathering. Describing the experience as a "turning point" in his life, John Till would go on to become team captain of the 1962 squad. For Till, his success in getting all the boys to stay at camp gave him his first boost of confidence "as a leader of his class and team." Till attributes many of the lessons learned from Coach Thorn and Headland football as the reason he was successful in his future endeavors at the US

Naval Academy, and his subsequent career as a pioneer in the study of radioactive materials.

Following camp, with optimally conditioned bodies and minds, the Headland Highlanders were ready. Or almost ready. Despite their mental and physical toughness, the Highlanders still had several challenges to overcome. "They're not very big" was a common critique of the team. This was true: The majority of boys fell in the roughly five feet, eight inches category, with quarterback Larry Carter weighing in at a wiry 125 pounds. The roster didn't carry any "star" athletes either. This wasn't a problem for Bill. Instead, it presented an opportunity for him to show off his coaching ingenuity. In the days before film and internet searches, Bill would create comprehensive scouting reports on each and every opponent, featuring a diagram of every play, in addition to every player's height, weight, and story.

The team also relied on a very small playbook—but out of the plays they had, they knew how to run them well. "We had maybe ten different plays and only five that really worked. So five on the left, which could be reversed to the right," recalled one former Highlander.

Even with a small playbook and a smaller, more demure force, this preparation—physically and mentally—led the Headland boys to see success. As Till recalled, "The students were hard workers, not star athletes. But Coach could make the whole team more than the sum of its parts." For each game, the stakes were high, and the motive was unspoken: The boys knew the price they'd already paid to get there, and it was time to reap the rewards of a summer of sweaty two-a-day workouts and a year of virtually no days off. As Mike Mitchell recalled, most games were won in the fourth quarter. "We'd come from behind. They would make mistakes, and we wouldn't. They would get tired, and we'd make a play. And it just kept building and building."

Plus, Bill always kept a few tricks up his sleeve, frequently going for fourth downs and trick plays. According to him, "When you're out-talented, you have to compete and find some way to stay in the game, right?"

John Till and Coach Thorn, 2014

Captain of the 1962 Headland Highlanders football team, John Till would go on to earn an appointment to the US Naval Academy in 1963, followed by a commission into the Navy Nuclear Submarine Officer Program in 1967.

Following his active-duty service, Till received his MS degree from Colorado State University in 1972 and his PhD from the Georgia Institute of Technology in 1976. In 1977, he formed the Risk Assessment Corporation (RAC). Since its formation, RAC has played a key role in the understanding of radioactive materials when they enter the environment and their subsequent effect on humans. For his contributions within the scientific and health fields, Dr. Till has been awarded numerous honors, including the E. O. Lawrence Award from the US Department of Energy, the L. S. Taylor Medal from the National Council on Radiation Protection and Measurements, and the Health Physics Society's Distinguished Scientific Achievement Award.

Dr. Till remained in the US Navy Reserve following his active-duty service and retired as a decorated Rear Admiral in 1999. His many military accolades include the Department of Defense Distinguished Service Medal, the Legion of Merit, two Navy Meritorious Service Medals, two Navy Commendation Medals, and the Navy Achievement Medal.

The kids dug even deeper to impress Bill. "You didn't want to admit you were hurt or struggling, because you didn't want to fall out of favor," admitted Mike Elsberry, who played quarterback with a broken tibia during a particularly momentous game against Russell High School. "I didn't want to let Coach down. The doctor used half of a cardboard tape tube as a makeshift splint, and we went on to beat Russell High School 15-13."

Losses weren't lamented or punished. After all, an undersized squad who found success through outworking, outhustling, and outlasting their rivals were inevitably bound to find an adversary with comparable levels of stamina—*and* more weight or talent on their roster. So when the 1962 Headland Highlanders Football team finished their season (and Bill's second as head coach) with a record of 9-2, Bill summed up the greatness of his team: "I think we could have won the quarterfinal game. But at the same time, we took that talent level as far as anybody could have possibly expected it to go." Headland outscored their opponents 176–60 that season, with four shutouts from their defense (who averaged 6.6 points per game allowed) and only one shutout on their offense (averaging 19.5 points per game).

Coach Thorn always said, "I never cut anybody from my football or track teams. Regardless of talent, you had the opportunity to play for me." I finished that thought with, "Yeah, but you have to commit to all the work and effort demanded, or you wouldn't be out here."

—Mike Mitchell, Headland High School football and track athlete

And that, ultimately, was what many alumni would say defined the Headland years and set the stage for a toughness the players would carry for the rest of their lives. However, the unrelenting grit they developed working for Bill isn't the only thing they carried; on top of preaching mental fortitude and determination, he began sharing who God was to his players.

Mike Elsberry and Coach Thorn, 1964

Something had shifted in Bill. Though he'd always been aware of God, grown up in a Methodist household, and even attended seminary at Emory University for a semester, Bill didn't really *know* God. He had not given his life over to Christ yet; he didn't view Jesus as his Savior and he wasn't looking to God for all his answers.

But in those last few years at Headland, he began to.

Patty—who had grown up Episcopalian and accepted Christ as a young schoolgirl but had not matured in her faith since then—started attending a women's Bible study and developed what Reverend Howard Dial called "a personal relationship with the Lord."

Patty urged Bill to attend a Bible study her friend had arranged for the husbands of women from her own study. Bill started attending, and one night, it all aligned; Bill went into his bedroom, got down on his knees, and asked the Lord to be his Savior. He invited God into his heart and began a lifelong, personal relationship with Christ. And from that moment on, every part of his life was different.

"Bill is a man that doesn't look back," Reverend Dial said. "To use a track metaphor, he went right out of the starting blocks. He wanted to know scriptures; he was determined to be a witness to the Gospel wherever he was and in whatever he was doing."

When Bill talked with people, he was never ashamed to bring up the Gospel. When you talked with Bill, you knew you were around a godly man. "Bill wasn't the man who showed up pious on Sundays and then went on with his week," Reverend Dial said. That just wasn't Bill.

Bill's relationship with the Lord didn't change his tough approach to coaching—but it did help players better understand the root of his tough love.

"Before Bill was saved, he was a no-nonsense guy," Reverend Dial said. "Christ came into his life—and he was still no-nonsense. But he was compassionate too."

As Mike Mitchell explained, "At the time, it didn't seem like there was a lot of love or sympathy in the process. But when you look back, you see that there was. It was a tough, Christian love: You had to put yourself second and put the objective of the team first."

His pep talks were still peppered with discussions of mental toughness—but now, they were peppered with something else too. Bill talked about God with his players. Every time the team circled up, something would always come back to the Lord.

As it turns out, Bill's calling wasn't coaching; his passion was. It was his *calling* to share the Gospel with every player and coach he worked with—a calling that would carry him through Headland, business ventures, and other schools to come.

Bill's time at Headland High School wasn't adorned with a state championship. It isn't the period of coaching that contributes most to his winning legacy or State of Georgia records. However, his decade-long tenure solidified Bill's reputation as a winning coach and truly held something special.

As recounted by Mike Mitchell, while Coach Thorn was at Headland, he "was one of the winningest coaches in the Greater Atlanta Area for his ten years. And yet, he only won one playoff game. It still didn't take away from him what he had on that program and on the kids who played for him. And so, the idea of state championships, that's really a nice thing . . . But from my perspective, that really wasn't a measure for him. I just remember the impact he had on the kids. And how long it's just stayed with you through time."

My father, Lamar Seals, and Coach Thorn were coaches at Headland High School in East Point together. My first introduction to Coach Thorn, Mrs. Patty, and their family was at their home when I was a child. The Thorns had horses, and we enjoyed a wonderful day riding (or, in this case, as a small child, being led around the ring). At this time, my father had left coaching, but the stories my father shared of Coach Thorn when I was young accurately reflected the man that my own children would call Coach Thorn. Coach is a man of his word. He is old-school and results driven. He requires much, but he gives even more. He loves fiercely and he would give you the shirt off his back. His love for Christ is as real and authentic as his love for his family. Our family has been blessed by his friendship, and his impact on our lives will always be cherished.

—Lorri Swords, Thorn family friend

The Headland Coaching Years Recap:

8 years as Head Football Coach

2 years as Assistant Football Coach

Record: 60-23-3

3 region runner-up titles

2 region championships

2 state quarterfinalist appearances

2 Coach of the Year Awards (1967, 1968 GHSA Regional Coach of the Year)

8 years as Head Track Coach

2 years as Assistant Track Coach

1963 Regional Track Coach of the Year

1963-1969 Regional Track Chairman

4 region championships

2 state runner-up titles

4 region Coach of the Year Awards

2 state champion titles

1 year as Head Soccer Coach

4 years as Athletic Director

Region 2AA Coaches of the Year

Baseball coach of the Headland Highlanders, Jack Short was named 2AA Baseball coach of the year. Jack's Highlanders compiled a season record of [illegible], winning [illegible] games for the Region Championship. They also made a determined bid for the State Crown, — winning 1 and losing in one in the finals. Jack attended Western Carolina and is an active member of the Fellowship of Christian Athletes at Headland High and also in this area.

COACH JACK SHORT

Bill Thorn, coach of Headland's Cindermen, has been named Region 2AA Coach of the year on the strength of his team's undefeated season, with an outstanding record of 7-0, winning the Region title and going on to win the First Annual Tri-City Relays. He is also the head coach of football whose team won the sub-region championship. Bill attended Birmingham Southern and is an active member of the Fellowship of Christian Athletes at Headland and in this area.

BILL THORN

Jubilant Headland Coach Bill Thorn is carried from field by equally jubilant team following Region 2-AA win.

Additional photos from Coach Thorn's Headland coaching years

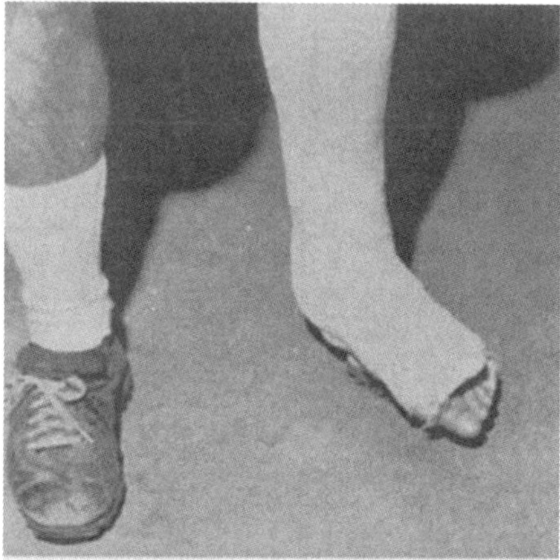

Coach Thorn rules with an iron hand and a plaster foot.

Additional photos from Coach Thorn's Headland coaching years

FIVE

"WINNERS FIND A WAY, AND LOSERS FIND A WAY OUT" —THORNISM

WE'RE ALWAYS AT THE MERCY of what we perceive to be our own limitations. As humans, we're often hindered by self-doubt, self-denial, and—in many ways—self-preservation. We tell lies and victimize ourselves to protect ourselves from struggle and potential failure.

Bill was known for a different mindset—one that he used with his football players and runners to show them that determination and persistence always win out in the end.

It wasn't just something he said for the sake of saying it. It was something he knew—from experience, from practice, and from putting his own head down and getting to work. It was a phrase with an implication that showed up in everything he did.

Winners find a way.

While Bill knew that coaching was his passion, he also knew the salary alone was not enough to take care of his growing family. With his father's words "You can have anything you want as long as you can pay for it" becoming an ever louder echo in his mind, Bill felt pulled to try a different career to provide a better life for his family. As Bill said, "Don't get into coaching unless you can satisfy the needs of your family," and after a decade of coaching at Headland, Bill needed to explore other opportunities to satisfy those needs.

Before ultimately deciding to step back from coaching following his tenure at Headland, Bill had already started pursuing supplemental forms of income while living frugally to stretch his coach's pay. When one of Bill's friends started selling life insurance, Bill helped him sell a few policies.

Bill also sought mentorship and learned from the success of others. While at GMA, Bill started learning about profitable opportunities in real estate from a longtime recruiter at GMA, Colonel Manchester "Ben" Paget. Colonel Paget mentored Bill in the real estate market, recognizing how Bill's frugal nature would be key in providing a good living for his young family. He encouraged Bill to invest in property while still young so he could start building long-term, stable wealth (like he himself had done in the College Park area).

There's a saying Bill knew and abided by—one he would continue to abide by in his later years of coaching: *He who can't be advised can't be helped.* Bill wanted help, was open to learning from Colonel Paget, and took his advice to heart.

Bill's property and real estate philosophy was a lot like his coaching philosophy: Get the fundamentals straight in the beginning, follow them, and don't let anything distract you. Do things that way, he thought, and he'd make investment strides quickly.

By the time he would leave GMA, Bill would own and rent out his first quadruplex in College Park, Georgia, and began seeking ways to continue maximizing income on his properties.

Plus, a dose of necessity provided Bill with experience in construction. When he left GMA, it meant leaving the free room and board at the on-campus dormitories. So Bill, Patty, and the girls found a tiny home on Ben Hill Road in East Point, Georgia, to purchase. For a total of 11,000 dollars, paid off in fifty-three-dollar notes per month, the two-bedroom home was just enough for Bill and Patty to share one bedroom and Lynn and Cheryl to share the other.

However, the family of four wouldn't stay a family of four for long. In the fall of 1959, during Bill's first season at Headland High School as an assistant coach, William "Bill" Thorn Jr. was born. While the girls had arrived in May and June of their respective years, Bill Jr. entered the world on a Thursday in the midst of a Headland High School football season. Bill's team, excited for their coach's first son, gifted him the winning game ball the following night (because, of course, Bill had no plans to miss the game).

Thorn Family Christmas card, 1960

While the first thought upon Patty's pregnancy with Lynn was, "How are we going to afford this baby?" the first thought upon Bill Jr.'s arrival was, "Where are we going to *put* this baby?" So Bill honed his construction skills (something he would use heavily in the coming years) and enclosed the outside porch of their two-bedroom home, making a new room for his new son. Bill's frugalness and skilled craftmanship became integral again four years later when the Thorns' fourth child, a son named Terry, made a surprise entrance. Without space to build another room for the house, Bill devised the perfect solution for their expanding family: Bill found bunk beds for the back porch room.

When asked if he attended the Friday night game the following day after Bill Jr.'s birth, Patty smiled: "He doesn't miss a game!" The game, ironically, would end up being against Campbell-Fairburn at the stadium that would—decades later— be named in Bill's honor.

All four Thorn children, 1964

Alongside his ventures in real estate and construction, another opportunity outside of coaching arose for Bill in the '60s while he was coaching at Headland. Bill's older cousin Alvin Miller told Bill about his new architectural invention at a chance encounter while both men were attending a family funeral. Alvin, who had settled in Arizona following military service in World War II, had designed a unique, twelve-sided, prefabricated house that he named a "Rondette." With a patented, unique cabling system for the structure's roof, the house was designed to withstand seventy-plus mile-per-hour winds and could be ordered for delivery from a catalog. The customer would receive the prepackaged house in "twelve slices" that could be put together "like a pie."

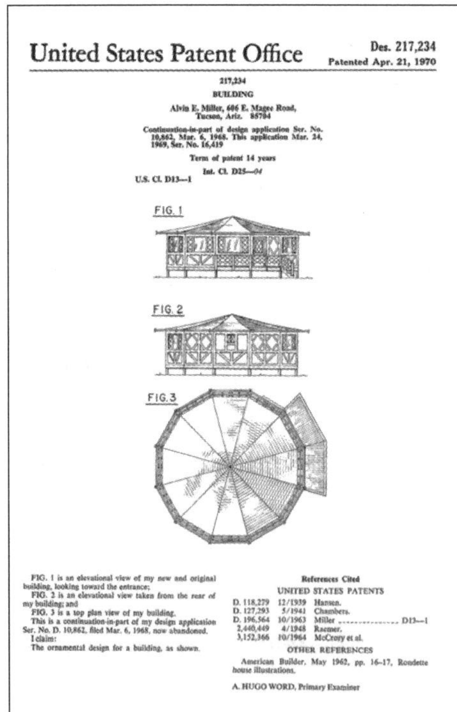

United States Patent Office — Des. 217,234 — Patented Apr. 21, 1970

217,234
BUILDING
Alvin E. Miller, 606 E. Magee Road, Tucson, Ariz. 85704
Continuation-in-part of design application Ser. No. 10,862, Mar. 6, 1968. This application Mar. 24, 1969, Ser. No. 16,419
Term of patent 14 years
Int. Cl. D25—04
U.S. Cl. D13—1

FIG. 1

FIG. 2

FIG. 3

FIG. 1 is an elevational view of my new and original building, looking toward the entrance;
FIG. 2 is an elevational view taken from the rear of my building; and
FIG. 3 is a top plan view of my building.
This is a continuation-in-part of my design application Ser. No. D. 10,862, filed Mar. 6, 1968, now abandoned.
I claim:
The ornamental design for a building, as shown.

References Cited
UNITED STATES PATENTS

D. 118,279	12/1939	Hansen.	
D. 127,293	5/1941	Chambers.	
D. 196,564	10/1963	Miller	D13—1
2,440,449	4/1948	Raemer.	
3,152,366	10/1964	McCrory et al.	

OTHER REFERENCES
American Builder, May 1962, pp. 16–17, Rondette house illustrations.

A. HUGO WORD, Primary Examiner

Design patent for the Rondette

Intrigued by the possibility of constructing his own house, Bill purchased one of the Rondettes at a family discount price from the factory in Asheville, North Carolina. Fortuitously, at the same time Bill purchased the Rondette, Bill's father-in-law, Clanton Walton, had recently returned from a fishing trip to Gulf Shores, Alabama, with tales of countless open lots for sale. Seeing the writing on the wall that the quiet beachfront area of Gulf Shores was about to explode for tourism, Clanton and his friend purchased side-by-side lots in the most popular area of Gulf Shores, beside mom-and-pop motels and a sprawling Holiday Inn. Bill hatched a plan: He would build his Rondette in Gulf Shores and rent it out for extra income.

With the help of a trusted carpenter, Bill got to work. His father-in-law contributed the lot, and Bill contributed the know-how and the labor. Together, the two men would split the construction cost of materials and would share the eventual home as both a vacation home and rental property. The finished home featured five rooms: two bedrooms, a living room, a kitchen, and a bathroom. While Rondettes were normally built on a slab or crawl space, Bill built his on an elevated foundation of cinder blocks so the twelve-sided building now had two stories, doubling its normal size. Frequented by Bill's family, in-laws, and friends, the Rondette became both a loved family vacation home and a valuable source of investment property and rental income.

The Rondette Bill hand-built

The potential for Gulf Shores and the Rondette seemed truly limitless until Hurricane Frederic hit in 1979. After an onslaught of damage throughout Puerto Rico, the US Virgin Islands, and much of the Caribbean, Frederic reached the US mainland in early September.

It was, at the time, the costliest tropical cyclone in recorded history, inflicting damages totaling nearly two billion USD (equivalent to more than 8.6 billion by 2024). As seventy miles-per-hour winds ripped ashore, beachfront properties up and down the Gulf were completely leveled. The entire middle of the Holiday Inn was wiped out, as was an entire unit of apartments next door to Bill's Rondette. Some investors lost their lots, sand and all. Amidst the chaos and destruction, however, the Rondette stood strong, with only one window knocked out.

Real estate nationwide was booming back then, and—as is the case following natural disasters and devastation—investors soon homed in on the Gulf Shores area like vultures. Property owners in Gulf Shores started to pick up the pieces and rebuild. The Holiday Inn was rebuilt, too, and looked to Bill's lot across the street to expand with additional parking and tennis courts. After striking a deal, Bill relinquished the property, but the Rondette survived to live another day. As Bill recounted, "The hotel had the means to move the house, so they didn't destroy it. I've been told by various people they've seen it somewhere, here, or there."

That wasn't the end of Bill's investments in Gulf Shores, however. Prior to Frederic, there were a variety of individual homes built behind sand dunes and only a single condominium complex on Gulf Shores. Afterward, hundreds of high-rises sprung up like weeds, and Bill decided to continue investing in the Gulf Shores area. He made a steady income buying low and selling high, all while living modestly. One such deal in the mid-'80s featured an eighty-acre lot along the main Fort Morgan Highway leading out to Mobile Bay. Selling for 150,000 dollars with 10 percent down and ten years to pay it off, Bill convinced ten people he knew to put down about two grand each. A year later, the group voted (or outvoted Bill) to sell . . . each investor doubling their money.

With his toes already soaking wet in the game in Alabama, Bill decided to get his real estate broker's license on his home turf in Georgia, passing the exam on his first try. With his license, Bill officially formed Thorn Realty and Coach's Construction.

However, two businesses weren't enough for hungry and hustling Bill. After leasing an old Sinclair gas station on Main Street in College Park, Bill started yet another new venture: Coach's Tires. For five years, Bill would change oil, sell tires, and—most profitably—tow cars for auto dealers' trade-ins. As an extra source of income, Bill would buy a few of the trade-ins he towed and fix the cars up, selling them for profit on his lot.

Between his three businesses, Bill was a scouting, building, and reselling machine—both for profit and for friends. When Bill's close friend, Bible study leader, running partner, and eventual pastor, Howard Dial, chose to leave a church that wouldn't accept African American members, Bill helped him find a property to start a church of his own—and helped him build it: an old-fashioned, barn-style building, built completely debt-free through their own labor and attendees' funding. In 1986, when Howard and his wife found themselves short on cash, Bill also helped them build a house, at cost, on a vacant lot Bill had developed in a subdivision.

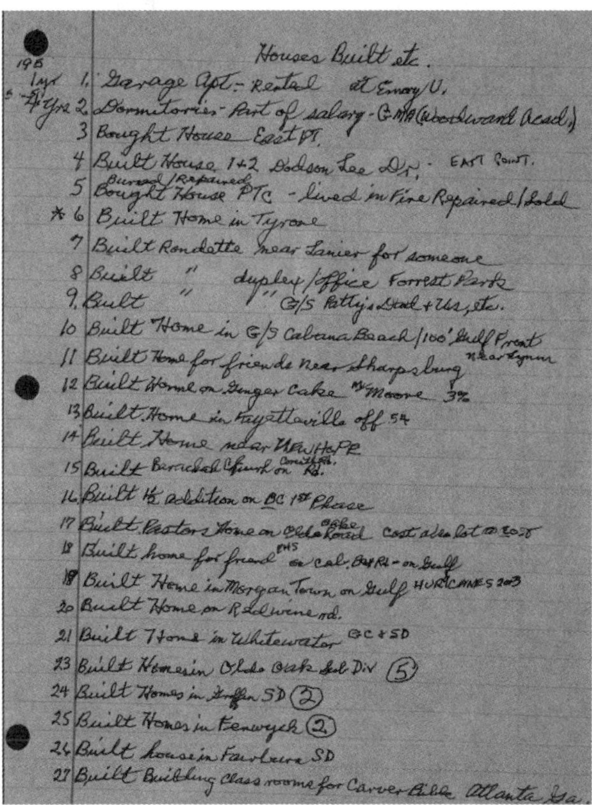
Houses Built etc.
1 yr 1. Garage Apt. - Rental at Emory U.
4 yrs 2. Dormitories - Part of salary - GMA (Woodward Acad.)
3 Bought House East PT.
4 Built House 1+2 Dodson Lee Dr. - EAST POINT.
5 Bought House PTC - lived in Fire Repaired/Sold
* 6 Built Home in Tyrone
7 Built Rondette near Lanier for someone
8 Built " duplex/office Forrest Park
9. Built " " G/S Patty's Dad + Us, etc.
10 Built Home in G/S Cabana Beach/100' Gulf Front
11 Built Home for friends near Sharpsburg near Lynn
12 Built Home on Ginger Cake Mr Moore 3%
13 Built Home in Fayetteville off 54
14 Built Home near NEW HOPE
15 Built [illegible] Church on [illegible] Rd.
16 Built ½ addition on BC 1st Phase
17 Built Pastors Home on Olde Road cost also lot [illegible]
18 Built home for friend on Cal. Bay Rd - on Gulf
19 Built Home in Morgan Town on Gulf HURICANES 2003
20 Built Home on Redwine rd.
21 Built 7 Home in Whitewater BC + SD
23 Built Homes in Olde Oak Sub Div (5)
24 Built Homes in [illegible] SD (2)
25 Built Homes in Fenwyck (2)
26 Built house in Fairlane SD
27 Built Building Class rooms for Carver Bible Atlanta Ga.

Bill's personal list of houses he built

Amid buying and selling down on the Guf, visiting on weekends and whenever time permitted between coaching obligations, real estate in the North Georgia mountains also caught Bill's eye. He bought land at 250 dollars per acre with three friends—David Jimmerson, Bill Dixon, and Buck Tallman—and dabbled in developing but eventually resold the land for a healthy profit years later.

Outside of building financial investments, Bill also started investing more in his physical health. He had always been an athlete, but with his football days as a player well behind him, Bill focused on a new personal sport: running. Inspired by Ken Cooper's book *Aerobics,* Bill began to train for distance running. Possibly with some divine timing, Bill's burgeoning passion came at the same time as the emergence of a new event in Atlanta: the Peachtree 10K Road Race. (But more to come on this later!)

Bill's investment philosophy, business philosophy, coaching philosophy, personal physical fitness philosophy, and even his life philosophy were built on the same foundation—good character. To Bill, good character was the beginning and end of any discussion about how to behave, think, or act and one of the most important building blocks of mental toughness.

And mental toughness, as Howard said, is what everyone needs to weather any storm.

STATE OF GEORGIA
REAL ESTATE COMMISSION

WILLIAM JACKSON THORN

5139

IS AUTHORIZED TO TRANSACT BUSINESS IN GEORGIA AS A LICENSED

BROKER

THE PRIVILEGE AND RESPONSIBILITIES OF THIS LICENSURE SHALL CONTINUE IN EFFECT AS LONG AS THE LICENSEE PAYS REQUIRED LICENSE FEES AND COMPLIES WITH ALL OTHER REQUIREMENTS OF THE OFFICIAL CODE OF GEORGIA ANNOTATED, CHAPTER 43-40. THE LICENSEE IS SOLELY RESPONSIBLE FOR THE PAYMENT OF ALL FEES ON A TIMELY BASIS.

CLAYTON FOSTER
Chairperson

JERRY WARSHAW
Vice Chairperson

PAUL G. BROWER
DAVID J. BURGE
CINDY RAMPLEY
JODIE SHEPARD

Bill's real estate broker's license

SIX

"HARD WORK TAKES TALENT TO A HIGHER LEVEL—BUT SMART WORK, GIVEN TIME, DEFEATS TALENT"

—MARSHALL SELLERS, PAAVO CAMPS

WHEN BILL LEFT HEADLAND HIGH SCHOOL in 1969, he left coaching—but only temporarily. After an approximately decade-long hiatus, Bill found his way back to the field. Or rather, the field found Bill.

Colonial Hills Christian School athletics was in dire straits. After achieving football success in the '70s with playoff runs and a state championship in 1977, the tide had turned. Disciplinary problems ravaged the seniors, leadership was lackluster at best, and the once-dominant football program was in need of a total overhaul.

On the verge of "scrapping" the entire program, school administrators walked a few blocks down the street to Coach's Tires and found Bill. Looking for a "body" to turn the program around and aware of Bill's success at Headland, they convinced Bill to return to coaching. In the spring of 1981, Bill was a head football coach again.

Bill, who never took any job less than seriously, began his overhaul of the program immediately by hosting a lunchroom meeting for prospective players. David Wilkins, a sophomore at the time, was in that first meeting.

"I had an idea of what a football coach was . . . basically, *mean*," he recalled. "But then in comes this little, short fella with white hair. He was very direct. I knew he meant business and wasn't there to mollycoddle anybody. He said, 'I'm not going to cut anybody; you're going to cut yourself.'"

As a rising tenth-grader who had never played football before, that statement appealed to Wilkins. "I knew if I stayed and did the right things, I might actually have a chance at playing some football."

Although Bill's words held true throughout his entire coaching career, they were especially true at Colonial Hills: He didn't have the numbers to cut anybody. After all, only eight players showed up for their first meeting.

Bill was scrappy, but nonetheless realistic. "That's not going to make a team," he told the school, to which they responded, "We have another meeting scheduled. Come on back—there will be more."

"More," as it turned out, entailed only two additional boys.

Coach Thorn on the sidelines (photo courtesy of David Wilkins)

By the time the season was ready to begin, the roster totaled only about fifteen boys—many of whom were seniors "not used to working hard, who feigned a lot of injuries." This was in stark contrast to most of their opponents they would soon face, who could fill the sidelines with fifty or sixty rough-and-ready teens.

Talent was a nice thing to have on your team, but to Bill, hard work always won out in the end. He'd seen it work at Headland; why couldn't the same fate occur at Colonial Hills?

Bill knew they had their work cut out for them and began this work at their first summer camp. "We looked like a bunch of hoboes, wearing whatever we could find," Wilkins recalled. Bill eventually made arrangements to obtain practice jerseys from schools in the area that had closed down, providing his players with a sort of uniform—albeit secondhand—to begin *looking* like as much of a team as they were becoming.

Practices began with the fundamentals. As Wilkins described it, "Most coaches take good players and coach them well. Bill Thorn would take kids who didn't know anything and couldn't walk straight and turn them into athletes. He taught us how to run. He would say, 'This is the way you run; this is how you put your feet. This is how you swing your arms: You don't cross your body, you put your arms parallel and you move yourself forward.'" Bill also incorporated a "bigger, faster, stronger" Program, which introduced weight-lifting regimens Bill had learned about in a local Lake City gym.

Bill's "revolutionary" weight-lifting regimen was something few other teams did. After all, Bill had the players lifting weights "before weights were cool," but Bill knew the conditioning benefits of weight-lifting would be very visible on the field.

However, finding a space for practices and games proved nearly as difficult as Coach Thorn's training Program. Colonial Hills was located in East Point, in the heart of the city of Atlanta. Prior to Bill's tenure, the team practiced at Randall Field, which was a long drive from the school. While the older kids drove themselves, younger students squeezed onto a rusty old bus among the practice dummies, pads, and sleds they had to load for every practice. Upon arrival at Randall Field, the team unloaded and set up all their equipment and reversed the process once practice was complete. The time required to set up and break down equipment for every practice was exceptionally inefficient and a source of immediate frustration for Bill.

So he changed things up. The team began using a practice field adjacent to Colonial Hills, behind Jerry Wells Elementary School. Separated by a fence, the kids slung their pads, gear, and then themselves over the top until Bill whipped out his construction skills and built a swinging gate. For games, Bill employed his negotiation skills for a unique solution. Through an agreement with the City of East Point, Bill gained access to the abandoned stadium behind South Fulton High School, which had been closed as part of the desegregation of schools.

It was a rough field—complete with a grassless sandbar down the middle, only a few flickering stadium lights, and end zones littered with broken glass from beer bottles—but it was theirs, and it was home. "It was mostly gravel," recalled alum Jeff Doris, "and it left kids with scars."

Despite the conditions, Bill made the most of it—and didn't squander an opportunity to insert practices where he could. One week, the school sent students on a weeklong retreat to a Christian camp in North Carolina. The agenda involved exploring the area, seeing waterfalls, and relaxation—which the football players (especially) were eagerly anticipating.

"Hey, I'm coming too," Bill announced, almost as quickly as he could load the bus with tackling dummies and a busload of equipment.

Bill Thorn and Eric Dial prior to the 2019 Peachtree Road Race

Prior to playing for Coach Thorn on the football and track teams, Eric Dial knew Bill as an exceptionally "generous" man who cared deeply for the Dial family. Howard Dial, Eric's father, was Bill's longtime pastor and friend, but Eric got to see a different side of Bill when he started playing football and track under Coach Thorn's leadership at Colonial Hills. Instead of just seeing Bill as a family friend and coach, Eric came to see Bill as a missionary "in a field that really needed it." As Eric recounted, "Every single time there was an opportunity for us to learn life lessons, to learn biblical lessons, to mature as upcoming men, that was Bill's passion . . . every time there was an opportunity [to impart] life skills, he pounced right on it."

Following graduation from Colonial Hills, Eric earned a BA in political science from Georgia State University. After working in the office of US Representative Mac Collins, Eric formed Dial Strategic Consulting, a nonprofit consulting and government affairs firm located in Tyrone, Georgia. Elected to the town council in 2007, Eric was elected Mayor of Tyrone in 2012 and continues to serve in that position.

Eric Dial recalled the experience: "We're in the mountains. So what does a rowdy group of boys do in the mountains? Go off and see what kind of trouble they can cause. So we went out in the woods and just acted like idiots . . . and got lost. We found our way back and were late to practice. But Coach didn't punish us with running, or push-ups, or silly things like that. He sat us down and said, 'I'm going to let the guys who you let down punish you.' So our teammates who weren't late chose our punishment—a 'shuck drill,' in which we formed a line and just hit one another, laterally down the line. We weren't late to practice again after that."

The dedication to preparation—and the lessons learned along the way—would serve the kids well. When the 1981 season began, Doris noted, "We welcomed the games. Not because we had the opportunity to win, but because we got to actually play football and not run a marathon at practice."

Bill's coaching required seriousness at practices, and he expected the same on game days. Bill would quiet the team, subduing all whooping and hollering before the whistle even blew. "Cut it out and act like you've been here before," he'd say, before changing in the locker room and disappearing to run three to four miles on the other team's track before the game began.

Wilkins remembered, "Other teams would have fifty players, with matching cleats and matching socks, coming in on a big bus. We've got the Blue Bird Special from 1960, with maybe sixteen players dressed out. But we're not making any noise . . . We're very quiet . . . So when we scored and scored again, it was something to see."

Eric Dial corroborated the notion, recalling, "When we'd get off the bus, they'd say 'Oh, we got this.' And then you play, and suddenly it's, 'What are they feeding these people?' And what they were feeding them was Bill Thorn."

Although the scores weren't as frequent in Bill's first season—which wound up with a 3-5 record after starting 3-1—they set the stage for a momentum that would last through his tenure. One article from the time summed up the enthusiasm with the title, "Football Fever Won't Cool Off!" It read, "This season started a new chapter in Colonial Hills football! The team experienced a new spirit of togetherness as Bill impressed upon the players the importance of self-discipline."

"We won three games that year, which was probably three more than we won the previous year," recalled Doris. The three wins attracted a bigger turnout for the 1982 season—enough to start a JV program to serve as a scout team and feed kids to the varsity—but still nowhere near the size of their rivals' rosters. Most players would have to still play offense and defense, since the team only had nineteen on the varsity squad.

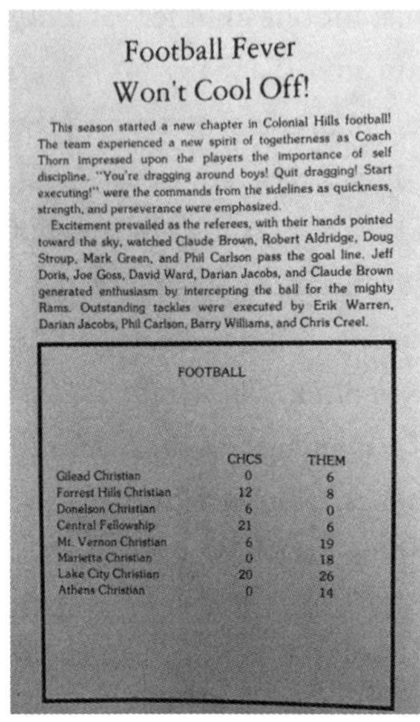

Football Fever Won't Cool Off!

This season started a new chapter in Colonial Hills football! The team experienced a new spirit of togetherness as Coach Thorn impressed upon the players the importance of self discipline. "You're dragging around boys! Quit dragging! Start executing!" were the commands from the sidelines as quickness, strength, and perseverance were emphasized.

Excitement prevailed as the referees, with their hands pointed toward the sky, watched Claude Brown, Robert Aldridge, Doug Stroup, Mark Green, and Phil Carlson pass the goal line. Jeff Doris, Joe Goss, David Ward, Darian Jacobs, and Claude Brown generated enthusiasm by intercepting the ball for the mighty Rams. Outstanding tackles were executed by Erik Warren, Darian Jacobs, Phil Carlson, Barry Williams, and Chris Creel.

FOOTBALL

	CHCS	THEM
Gilead Christian	0	6
Forrest Hills Christian	12	8
Donelson Christian	6	0
Central Fellowship	21	6
Mt. Vernon Christian	6	19
Marietta Christian	0	18
Lake City Christian	20	26
Athens Christian	0	14

Football fever press release

Nonetheless, Bill focused on quality over quantity. "They're a dedicated group of kids and they'll give you the effort. That's what it's all about," he told a local newspaper at the time.

Bill made additional adjustments after the first season: He set up a weight room for the kids to strength train, created a game-day eating program so that all players were adequately fueled, instituted a ten p.m. bedtime, and eliminated unnecessary distractions—including having the cheerleaders commute to away games on separate buses. The 1982 season featured almost all the same players, but they now boasted more strength, stamina, and solidarity.

However, an early game of the season against Forest Park didn't reflect the new-and-improved team. Bill—known for his resolute, calm, and quiet leadership—wasn't known to yell, cuss, throw clipboards, or lose his temper. His halftime talks were described as "businesslike," and he was noted by one alum as being "not much of a motivational speaker but could get to the heart of the matter pretty quick." So he expressed his disappointment to the team at halftime with a simple observation: "This is not what we've taught you. You've done this over the summer, and now you're just going through the motions. You're not cheating me; you're cheating yourselves."

Coach Thorn called the JV team "Teamers." I was not a good football player; I practiced pretty well, but I didn't apply what I learned on the practice field to the game field. The JV team practiced with the varsity team, and we got to hold the tackling dummies so the varsity could practice their plays. At the end of practice, Coach would gather both teams to talk. One time, Coach wasn't happy with some of the varsity players who had missed some practices. He started to look around at all of us players who took a knee to listen. He called out, "Hey . . . where's that Teamer . . . Wallace?" I raised my hand, and Coach told me to stand, and as I stood, he asked, "Hey, Teamer Wallace, how much did you play last game?" I answered, "A few minutes of the last quarter." Coach replied, "Son, how many practices have you missed?" "None, sir," was my reply. Coach then proceeded to chew out some of the varsity players for missing practices. I was convinced that I was a dead man in the locker room and in the halls of the school! For some reason, and I think Coach Thorn had something to do with it, I had some respect from the varsity players. The moment that Coach called me out is seared in my mind, and I will never forget it. Showing up and not quitting has stuck with me my whole life.

1982 CHCS "Teamers"

—Wilson Wallace, Colonial Hills High School athlete

The locker room was left in a state of quiet reflection. The boys got to work. Although they didn't come back to beat Forest Park in the first game of the season, the 1982 season turned into something legendary.

CHCS football team

The path wasn't easy, but it was smooth: after a 12-12 tie to Forrest Hills, a 26-12 win over Lake City, and their only loss of the season to Forest Park (7-6), the Rams started their championship roll with a decisive 21-6 victory over Central Fellowship. Visions of a championship began to implant in the Colonial Hills players' heads after another decisive win, 27-6, over defending state champions, Mt. Vernon. Mt. Vernon hadn't lost a game in four years, but through true physical grit on the ground and without completing a single pass, Colonial Hills dominated the clock and the scoreboard.

"Coach didn't use a playbook," Wilkins remembered. "He'd call a play from the sidelines, and we'd run it. We'd reset, and he'd call it again, and we'd run it again. Again, and again and again, until someone would say, 'Coach, they can hear you!' He'd retort, 'Well, they still gotta stop you. We'll run something different when they can stop this.'"

Their "sticking to what works" mentality led to the winning streak continuing over King's Way (35-0), Chapel Hill (29-3), Marietta Christian (25-0), and another game against Chapel Hill (38-13), putting the Rams at 7-1-1.

However, the highlight of their regular season was their homecoming matchup against Athens Christian. The rivalry was long-established, and both teams entered the game with impressive records. Colonial Hills came into the game on a six-game winning streak following their singular loss, and Athens Christian had an undefeated record of 6-0. However, the score didn't reflect much of an equal match, with the Rams making a statement to Athens Christian for scheduling them as their homecoming opponent with an emphatic 27-0 win.

After closing their regular season with a record of 8-1-1, the Rams' first game in the playoffs required facing a familiar foe: Forest Park, who had dealt them their only loss of the season. "We were younger then," Bill noted at the time, alluding to the maturity and momentum that a season together had bequeathed to his players.

After avenging their loss against Forest Park with a conclusive 26-6 triumph, Colonial Hills soon found themselves facing Athens Christian as their adversary once again—and, again, coming out on top. After a 7-6 victory due to a missed extra point, Colonial Hills was named the Georgia Athletic Christian Association (GACA) State Champions—Bill's first state championship in any sport.

CHCS track practice

All the hard work, all the pain, and all the determination Bill had pressed into the players had paid off. Many people questioned Bill when he had his players run miles on end as part of their conditioning. They looked at him like he was crazy when he tagged along on Christian camp trips to squeeze in a few more practices. The 10:00 p.m. bedtimes and meal plans might have seemed a little wild too.

But all the conditioning—all the discomfort, pain, and challenge—was the experience the boys needed for the moments leading to the state championship. "We just felt like we'd let him down," Doris said after the early loss to Forest Park. "So much, that we went on to win the state championship that year." With an impressive title and an overall record of 10-1-1, a local news outlet referred to the Colonial Hills team as a "Cinderella team of

1982" that had more than just talent, technique, or ambition—they had persistence in the pursuit of a dream.

If he could get them to show up and experience that discomfort and push through it all, and if he could just teach them how to succeed under pressure and work hard, despite what they were going through, they'd understand that eventually, it would all pay off.

There's a point in teaching and coaching, Bill said, where your players realize that everything they've put into it, all the buying into the belief and doing the things asked of them, eventually points them to success. The 1982 season was the success the boys had been chasing—it was the success that Bill knew they could achieve if they made it through the tough stuff. But the challenges didn't disappear once Colonial Hills won the state championship.

CHCS football team after winning the 1982 state championship

Following the success of their 1982 season, Bill and his boys faced two main challenges: First, no teams wanted to play them. Twice-defeated Athens Christian refused, so Bill took his boys all around the southeast and beyond—from Savannah to Hammond, Indiana—to garner some competition.

The second challenge arose from the classroom, with grade checks dwindling the roster even further. The quarterback, two tailbacks, and the kicker were forced to miss games with a sub-C grade point average, leaving the team with only thirteen players who had to play offense, defense, and special teams. Referees were known to remark when they took tally that the correct number of men were playing, not by counting the players on the field, but by simply counting the two standing by Bill's side.

Despite the numbers, their grit prevailed once again, earning the 1983 team a 9-1 season—their only loss coming on the last game of the season playing Maranatha Christian Academy from Florida in the championship game.

The following year, in 1984, the greatness would continue—with some fun along the way. On their field trip to face Bible Baptist down in Savannah, the team traveled by yellow school bus and booked a block of motel rooms on Abercorn Street. The players stayed four to a room, with David Wilkins' room comprised of three other senior linebackers and a room down the hall full of running backs and the quarterback. Understandably, a healthy rivalry existed between the linemen (the "unsung heroes who toil in the trenches") and the backs. When the backs conned the motel maid into letting them into the linemen's room, they thought it would be funny to dumpster dive and fill their floor and tabletops with empty liquor and beer bottles. The linemen, never ones to be outdone, immediately came up with a plan for revenge—and they brought Bill in on their scheme. They told the team that Coach and the principal had found the remnants of alcohol and were furious. They claimed they'd been suspended from the game, and that the second-string, undersized underclassmen would be protecting the backs from the supersized defense of Bible Baptist. After some serious consultation, the backs eventually came clean about their entire ruse—only to be met with Bill's laughter and the linemen's smug sense of success.

Coach Thorn on the CHCS sidelines
(photo courtesy of David Wilkins)

With their impeccable training, positive mindsets, and sense of camaraderie, the Rams finished the 1984 regular season 8-1 and earned their second state championship. One year later, in 1985, the team experienced their first undefeated regular season, with a final record of 10-0. However, they lost the championship 31-14 against Independent Methodist.

Bill's reentry into coaching football left him with a 47-14-1 record, two state championships, and one runner-up title.

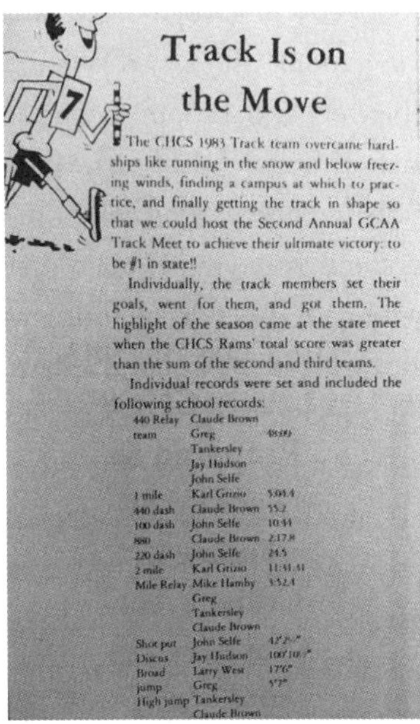

Track Is on the Move

The CHCS 1983 Track team overcame hardships like running in the snow and below freezing winds, finding a campus at which to practice, and finally getting the track in shape so that we could host the Second Annual GCAA Track Meet to achieve their ultimate victory: to be #1 in state!!

Individually, the track members set their goals, went for them, and got them. The highlight of the season came at the state meet when the CHCS Rams' total score was greater than the sum of the second and third teams.

Individual records were set and included the following school records:

440 Relay team	Claude Brown, Greg Tankersley, Jay Hudson, John Selfe	[illegible]
1 mile	Karl Grizio	5:04.4
440 dash	Claude Brown	55.2
100 dash	John Selfe	10.44
880	Claude Brown	2:17.8
220 dash	John Selfe	24.5
2 mile	Karl Grizio	11:51.51
Mile Relay	Mike Hamby, Greg Tankersley, Claude Brown	3:52.4
Shot put	John Selfe	[illegible]
Discus	Jay Hudson	[illegible]
Broad jump	Larry West	17'6"
High jump	Greg Tankersley, Claude Brown	5'7"

Track shout-out in the 1983 CHCS yearbook

However, football didn't provide the only trophies for Colonial Hills under Bill's leadership: Bill launched the track team in 1981, just in time for his football players to join in the offseason. The track team struggled with many of the problems the football program faced: no campus at which to practice, no track in shape enough to hold meets, and plenty of days of below-freezing temperatures.

However, also like the football boys, the track team found success by sticking to "The Program." In four seasons, the team won two state championships and one runner-up title. In 1983, the team was so dominant at the state meet that their total score was greater than the sum of the second- and third-place teams combined!

Perhaps one article from the Encounter Yearbook awards ceremony in 1986 summarizes Bill's achievements best: "It is from [Bill Thorn's] devotion to the sports that the CHCS trophy case is filled with first place prizes . . . It is easy to look at the great athletes who have played under Coach Thorn and focus on them alone, but we must not forget the coach who has put them together to make them the great teams they are."

In just a few years, Bill had gone from building houses to building championship teams.

Colonial Hills was Bill's reentry to the coaching world. After a shaky start, his "can't-quit" determination led him and his teams to victory. And just as his athletes took these lessons and carried them with them through life, Bill learned lessons about coaching too.

EXTRA! EXTRA! READ ALL ABOUT IT!

The CHCS Times Honors Coach For Outstanding Leadership.

For the past five years Coach Bill Thorn has spent his time building houses and building the championship teams CHCS is proud of today! It is from his devotion to the sports that the CHCS trophy case is filled with first place prizes.

The Rams football team began its reputation at being a championship team in 1982 when they swept the GCAA with a 10-1 season. The following two seasons were completed with 10-1 records. In 1984 Coach Thorn led his fighting Rams to the Peachstate championship by defeating Bible Baptist with a final score of 32-14. Throughout the 1985 season the Rams finished with an undefeated 10-0 record, their first undefeated season.

The Track team was formed in 1982 by Coach Thorn. In four seasons the team has won three championships and one second place.

It is easy to look at the great athletes who have played under Coach Thorn and focus on them alone, but we must not forget the coach who has put them together to make the great teams they are.

This year we dedicate the 1986 Encounter to the man who has dedicated himself to us, Coach Thorn we Thank You!

The 1983 CHCS yearbook, The Encounter, *was dedicated to Coach Thorn for his accomplishments and leadership.*

He'd come back to coaching after years of absence, and he wasn't about to stop now.

The Colonial Hills Christian School Coaching Years Recap:

6 years as Head Football Coach

Record: 47-14-1

1 regional runner-up title

1 state runner-up title

2 state championships

6 years as Head Track Coach

2 state runner-up titles

2 state championships

Football Coach
Bill Thorn

Additional photos from Bill's coaching time at Colonial Hills Christian School

LEADERSHIP LESSONS OF BILL THORN

BY CHUCK CUSUMANO

COACH BILL THORN'S REMARKABLE LIFE and career exemplify leadership principles that today are taught by celebrated leadership authors and thinkers. Long before Jim Collins defined a "Level 5 Leader" as one who demonstrates exceptional humility coupled with unwavering resolve, Coach Thorn embodied this exact balance by quietly building champions without ever seeking personal acclaim. Similarly, before John Maxwell popularized the "Law of the Lid," asserting that an organization can rise no higher than its leader's own effectiveness, Coach Thorn intuitively raised his own "leadership lid," consistently pushing himself physically, mentally, and spiritually to set an example that his athletes and others could follow. His emphasis on accountability, discipline, and clarity resonates closely with Patrick Lencioni's assertion that teams require trust, healthy conflict, commitment, accountability, and a focus on collective results. Coach Thorn inherently understood and practiced these principles, emphasizing integrity, personal responsibility, and clarity of expectations to achieve extraordinary results.

Moreover, Coach Thorn instinctively practiced servant leadership well before Robert Greenleaf defined it—always placing the needs, growth, and success of his athletes above personal glory, echoing the Biblical principle taught in Matthew 20:26: "Whoever wants to become great among you must be your servant." Coach Thorn's ability to build resilient teams that thrived through adversity closely mirrors Angela Duckworth's research on grit, demonstrating that passion and perseverance matter far more than talent alone. His coaching philosophy resonates deeply with Proverbs 27:17—"As iron sharpens iron, so one person sharpens another." Coach consistently challenged athletes to embrace difficulties as opportunities to grow stronger together.

Ultimately, Coach Thorn's life and "Thornisms" provide clear and profound examples of timeless leadership wisdom, principles that have since become pillars of modern leadership literature. Most of his athletes, when interviewed, said that Coach Thorn was doing this system or that program *before* it ever became mainstream or popular. Coach Thorn is an innovator and, when looking back on his legacy, you can see that he was one of the *originals*.

The following ten lessons are what we distilled from his extraordinary journey! They are practical, inspiring, and universally applicable. They offer valuable insights, whether you are pursuing personal growth or seeking guidance to lead, mentor, and coach others toward excellence. From a leadership and performance perspective, here is what we believe Coach Thorn would tell you if he were coaching you in your life today:

1. Persistence and Determination

Thornism: *"When it's hard to run, run hard."*

- For Yourself:
  - » Push through personal setbacks with determination, knowing challenges build resilience.
  - » Commit daily to activities that reinforce persistence, such as exercise, reading, consuming a healthy diet, or practicing skills.
- For Leading Others:
  - » Teach others to see obstacles as opportunities to build character.
  - » Praise and reward team members who demonstrate persistence, modeling the value of effort even during difficulty. Did you PR today?

2. Hard Work over Talent

Thornism: *"Hard work, over time, defeats talent or takes talent to a higher level."*

- For Yourself:
  - » Prioritize disciplined effort and practice over reliance on natural ability.

- » Embrace tasks that challenge you to work beyond your comfort zone, recognizing effort brings lasting results.
- » Go all out! Never leave anything for later.

- For Leading Others:
  - » Encourage your team by acknowledging effort and consistent improvement, not just inherent talent.
  - » Design training or development programs emphasizing steady progress and incremental improvement through deliberate practice.

3. Discipline and Accountability

Thornism: *"You can have anything you want in life, so long as you can pay for it."*

- For Yourself:
  - » Set clear, nonnegotiable personal standards, holding yourself accountable to achieving them.
  - » Regularly measure your progress, honestly assessing if you are putting in the necessary "payment" of time and effort.
  - » Record all of your activities so you can measure progress.
- For Leading Others:
  - » Clearly communicate expectations and consequences, teaching accountability through transparent, fair enforcement of standards.
  - » Create an environment where accountability is positively recognized as a pathway to success rather than punishment.

4. Individualized Development

Thornism: *"He who won't be advised can't be helped."*

- For Yourself:
  - » Actively seek and listen to constructive feedback from others, staying open and adaptable to new ideas.
  - » Personalize your own growth plan, acknowledging your unique strengths and weaknesses.
- For Leading Others:
  - » Invest time understanding each individual's motivations, strengths, and areas of improvement.

    - » Provide personalized mentoring and guidance, clearly communicating that openness to feedback is essential for growth.

5. Mental Toughness and Mindset

Thornism: *"If you think you are beaten, you are."*

- For Yourself:
    - » Maintain a positive, resilient mindset through consistent visualization and self-affirmation.
    - » Learn to quickly reframe setbacks as challenges that build toughness and character.
- For Leading Others:
    - » Teach your team to approach challenges with confidence and optimism, understanding their mindset directly shapes outcomes.
    - » Encourage resilience training and provide tools to help others manage stress, overcome anxiety, and persist through adversity.

6. Leading by Example

Thornism: *"'Play the game squarely' is one rule that will never be revised."*

- For Yourself:
    - » Consistently demonstrate integrity, fairness, and disciplined behavior, especially when nobody is watching.
    - » Lead by example in challenging situations, demonstrating composure, honesty, and resilience.
- For Leading Others:
    - » Model the behaviors and attitudes you want your team to adopt.
    - » Visibly participate in challenging tasks or situations, showing your commitment to shared standards and integrity.

7. Vision and Purpose

Thornism: *"Winners find a way, and losers find a way out."*

- For Yourself:
    - » Keep a clear vision and purpose, especially when facing obstacles, and commit yourself to finding solutions rather than excuses.

- » Regularly reflect on your "why" to stay motivated through challenging periods.
- For Leading Others:
  - » Clearly communicate and reinforce the overarching purpose and vision for your team or organization.
  - » Actively teach others to seek creative solutions rather than reasons to quit, using setbacks to strengthen their determination.

8. Integrity and Good Character

Thornism: *"A good disposition is important; all great players have it."*

- For Yourself:
  - » Prioritize personal integrity and character in every decision you make.
  - » Maintain a positive, humble disposition, regardless of external circumstances.
- For Leading Others:
  - » Emphasize and reward good character, humility, and integrity alongside achievement or performance.
  - » Consistently reinforce the idea that great teams and leaders must have positive, dependable character above mere talent.

9. Servant Leadership

Thornism: *"Your teammates keep your opponents off your neck."*

- For Yourself:
  - » Adopt a mindset focused on serving others, prioritizing collective success over personal gain.
  - » Frequently ask yourself, "How can I best serve the people around me?"
- For Leading Others:
  - » Teach your team members that leadership is fundamentally about helping and empowering others.
  - » Encourage mutual support within your group, clearly communicating that serving others builds trust, strength, and success.

10. Legacy and Influence

Thornism: *"You don't have to run; you get to run."*

- For Yourself:
  - » Cultivate gratitude by regularly acknowledging the opportunities and privileges you have, rather than viewing tasks as obligations.
  - » Intentionally consider your long-term legacy and how your actions today affect others tomorrow.
- For Leading Others:
  - » Regularly remind your team to appreciate the opportunities they've been given, teaching them to see their work as meaningful and impactful.
  - » Emphasize building a lasting, positive legacy through daily interactions and decisions, guiding them to make choices that positively influence future generations.

By clearly distinguishing how each lesson can be applied both for your own self-improvement and in your role as a leader or coach to guide others, you can fully leverage Coach Bill Thorn's timeless insights, Thornisms, and proven leadership principles to inspire growth, achievement, and positive, enduring impact in every aspect of life!

SEVEN

"A GOOD DISPOSITION IS IMPORTANT; ALL GREAT PLAYERS HAVE IT"

—THORNISM

WHEN IT CAME TO BILL'S COACHING, there was no bending.

No matter where he coached, one of the things he'd end up being infamous for—aside from just his focus on running—was his unwillingness to budge on what he knew worked. He believed in hard work over everything, including talent.

He pressed his players to focus on consistency and longevity over quick fixes. He emphasized perfecting the basics instead of throwing in new, flashy plays or strategies. And he didn't just ask for his players' respect; his leadership quietly demanded it.

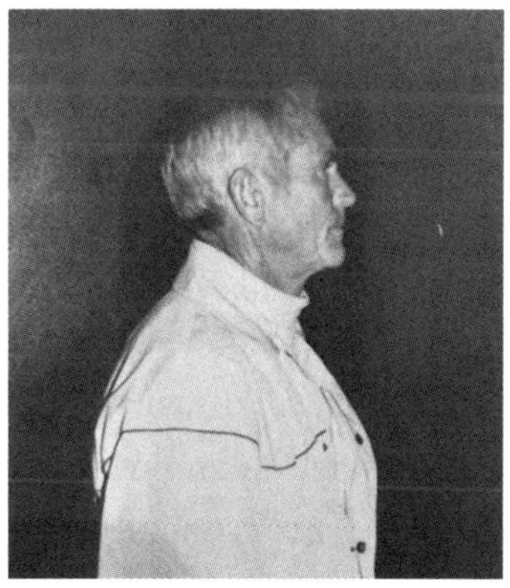

Coach Thorn at FCS (photo courtesy of David Harkins)

After experiencing substantial success at Colonial Hills, albeit with some friction from administration, Bill felt called to take on a new challenge, which led him to Fayette Christian School (FCS). The moment Bill accepted the head coaching position, and before he even stepped foot inside the halls at FCS, news of his reputation spread. "There was a lot of fear," said Roby Ross, who started playing for Bill during his junior year. "I'd heard other kids talk about running to death, so there was definitely fear."

Brad Waggoner agreed: "The first time I met Bill, I just remember he was a short guy with gray hair, and I was scared to death of him. But I also remember thinking, 'We're going to win with this coach.'"

Bill had his first opinions on the squad before him too: "When I first met the group, they were as scraggly looking as you can imagine . . . All sizes, all kinds."

That fear and uncertainty paved the path to a beautiful relationship. As Bill later reflected, "I was only there for two years, but there was something different about that group of kids."

The struggles to get the team up and running were reminiscent of those Bill had already faced and overcome at Headland and Colonial Hills alike: small rosters, equipment shortages, and—most importantly—lack of a place to practice.

But with Fayette Christian there was an additional hurdle to overcome: FCS had only ever played eight-man football. The 1987 season would be their first year playing eleven versus eleven.

With these challenges ahead, Bill set out to prepare the team. And for Bill, the best way to prepare was always running.

In the spring before his first season at Fayette Christian, Bill invited (although the RSVP wasn't so optional) the boys to join track practice at Colonial Hills. (Bill was still coaching at Colonial Hills then, so they allowed the FCS athletes to use their facilities.) Although getting the team on board mentally was only half the battle—physically getting the team to practice was the other. Fayette Christian had an old, green, beat-up "clunker that should have been in a trash pile" for transportation. It only fit fifteen kids, which was, luckily, enough to accommodate the entire roster.

Despite the running, the clunker, and the sudden shift in the program's direction, every member of the team was on board. "They came every single day without a person missing," Bill recalled. "They may have looked scraggly, but their enthusiasm was what impressed you."

There was something special about the way the Fayette Christian squad quickly took to Bill's coaching strategy. Because Bill's approach wasn't just about running faster, working harder, or lifting heavier—it was about doing all those things with the right mindset.

That mindset, though—that good disposition—would carry the team through even more challenges during their 1987 season.

> *People ask me all the time to describe Coach Thorn. I mean, he was tough. He cared about every single one of [his players], whether they were the best or worst on the team. He took pride in taking those kids that maybe . . . weren't the most talented and worked to improve [them]. It was all about improving. If we can improve, we're going to have a chance in the end. It's not where we start, but where you end. And that still sticks to me today.*
>
> *—Brad Waggoner, Fayette and Landmark Christian athlete*

Once track season came to an end, Bill needed to start the boys' football conditioning. But without being able to use Colonial Hill's campus, as Bill was no longer employed there, the team was at a loss. So in typical Bill fashion, he improvised and sourced the best option he could find: a plot of grass along Highway 314 next to a cement plant, on a vacant piece of land filled with "good-sized rocks" and surrounded by warehouse structures. With no locker rooms, the boys changed at the school or in their cars. With no lines or goalposts, the team innovated field markers. There was one faucet, which was used for an occasional water break or to clean out the inevitable cuts and scrapes kids endured from the rocky terrain.

Roby Ross, who had begun the season with fear, now had a new outlook: "When I started playing for him, I realized very quickly that it was what I'd been looking for. I wanted to have discipline, and I wanted to succeed, but I just didn't know the path. Other coaches abided by the attitude of either 'You're good or you're not.' But Bill laid out the steps to succeed. I was craving that, and it really helped change my whole life."

These are several of my favorite Coach Thorn memories:

Before my first ever track practice at FCS, I ate Froot Loops cereal and—after running, who knows how many "time laps"—I threw them up on the field. Coach Thorn laughed and called me "Froot Loop" for a good while after that.

At one of the more memorable football games, Coach Thorn went and sat on the bus at halftime because he was so disappointed in our effort level. After that, we played harder than ever before and won the game. Coach Thorn's response after the game was, "If you would have played like that in the first half, I could have watched the whole game."

He took me to many road races in the summers, and I was always amazed at how he would continue to run around the park after the race was over. I've never known anyone with more self-discipline in my life! I have coached for twenty years and still strive to have half the positive impact on my players that he had on me.

—Daniel Salvador, Fayette Christian and Landmark Christian athlete

With fear diminished and eyes on the prize, Fayette Christian's first game would prove to be a unique kind of test. Was the team's commitment, determination, and good disposition enough to push them toward victory? They'd be facing Colonial Hills, an opponent Bill tried to avoid because of his emotional connections to his most recent athletes. Despite his protests, the game remained on the schedule and resulted in Fayette Christian winning by an extra point. The boys celebrated "like they'd won a world championship." In their first year playing eleven-man football, they'd not only defeated a very recent state champion squad but went on to have a deep playoff run, where they only lost in the finals to Gilead Christian, ending the season with a 5-5 record but a state runner-up title.

The group headed into their second year under Bill with an even stronger thirst for the championship trophy and a willingness to put in the work to get there. That summer, David Harkins recalled a particular challenge: "Before the season started, we played two teams in the same week. We beat both teams, but we were run down in the second game. They still couldn't score on us, but we were running in slow motion. At the end of the second game, Coach said, 'I did this to you on purpose. I scheduled games back-to-back to see what kind of shape you guys were in . . . You worked your hearts out there and proved something to me.'"

As Bill would later comment, "I never really cared about winning. I just cared about people doing their absolute best and honoring God. If you do that, the winning takes care of itself."

And it certainly did. The wins came even more easily in Bill's second year at FCS, as the team "knew the system." After an initial loss to archrival Athens Christian (28-33) to start the season, the team posted four straight wins, including a 26-6 decisive win over Colonial Hills. However, a rematch in Macon against Gilead Christian on Gilead's homecoming night—a game scheduled by Gilead anticipating an easy win for the home team—proved a pivotal point in the middle of their season. Gilead had beaten Fayette Christian during the previous season twice—once in regular-season play and once in the championship—and was up 19-6 at halftime. Harkins recalled, "That score didn't even tell the whole story; they were just manhandling us. It was like David and Goliath out there. They were huge; we were not. We were intimidated." The Fayette Christian team still struggled with numbers, with a group of only twenty-five, where most kids played both offense and defense. Even the quarterback performed double duty as a free safety. Gilead, on the other hand, boasted a full sideline.

Coach Thorn had a way of knowing how to motivate each kid. He knew what made each kid tick. And so he knew how to get me to do whatever he wanted me to do—and everybody else on the team as well. But we weren't all the same. It's like your kids; your kids are all different. And he wasn't a "This is my way; you've got to do it this way" [type]. He knew how to get each kid and how to get the most out of each kid. And, looking back, that's probably the most amazing thing about him. He just had that innate sense about him.

It's amazing to see the impact that he had on the guys that he coached. I can name off several of the guys that I played with who are now coaches in high school because of him. And I can also name several guys that I played with that ended up writing an essay about him in college. Most of us had to write something on the topic of who is the most influential person in our life up to this point in college as a freshman, and all of us wrote about Coach Thorn—every last one of us. He just had that kind of an impact.

—David Harkins, Fayette Christian athlete

FCS football coaching staff
(photo courtesy of David Harkins)

At halftime, Bill uttered just one statement before leaving the locker room: "Boys," he said, "you're better than that. From now on and for the rest of your lives, you're going to have to remember that this team beat you three times in two years." The locker room doors clicked shut, leaving behind a state of complete silence. The captains remained quiet, and the others sat stewing, Bill's words ringing in their ears. As he'd always done, Bill cut right to the chase—no big speeches, no yelling or screaming. He didn't need to make a show of it; he just told the boys what they needed to hear.

FCS team after winning the state championship

With Bill's words on a broken record, the boys came back to win the game 44-31, outscoring Gilead 38-12 in the second half.

Following this come-from-behind victory, Fayette Christian successfully rolled through the rest of the year, which culminated in a 9-1 record and defeat of Westminster 13-0 in the state championship.

FCS football state championship team with Governor Joe Frank Harris

Two years of unbridled passion and dedicated practice had led to what the boys had dreamed of since their first ride in a "beat-up clunker" to track practice—a state championship. They were a testament to the fact that hard work paid off, heart mattered more than size, and that discipline could get them anywhere they desired to go. It was a magical group, and Bill had one thing to leave them with after the state championship: "You will never forget this time in your life."

FCS state championship celebration

Fayette Christian Coaching Recap:

2 years as Head Football Coach

Record 14-6

1 state runner-up title

1 state championship

1 year as Head Track Coach

EIGHT

"IT'S ONLY FOR THOSE WHO WILL DO IT"

—PAAVO RUNNING CAMP SLOGAN

WHEN ONE THINKS OF BILL THORN'S LEGACY, a few things may come to mind . . .

For one, his influence on the world through his influence on the next generation—the men and women who went on to become admirals, doctors, parents, teachers, and other coaches, largely thanks to a focus on self-discipline and hard work in their teenage years, and the alumni who credited Bill with helping get them through medical school, childbirth, or health battles, all because of learning the importance of mind over matter from their days in his locker room.

For others, his legacy is entrenched as a symbol of the Peachtree Road Race: a testament to the importance of taking care of your body so that you can still complete a 6.2-mile run in your nineties.

However, if one *school* were to serve as the crux of his legacy, it would have to be the one that he founded from scratch, that won more state titles than any other, and where the shadow of his name still shines proudly over the football field and track. That school would have to be Landmark Christian School.

The dream of forming Landmark began years before shovels hit dirt. The seed of the idea for a school with an emphasis on both the Bible and athletics—but that was not tied to the politics and policies of any particular church—had implanted in Bill's mind, and he engaged in casual conversations with others at his church who had similar ways of thinking. However, discussing a vision that would eventually blossom into a concrete idea proved to be two very different things, and it required a few changemakers coming on board to make things happen.

Those changemakers were Perry Duncan and Eddie Waggoner. The trio first met at a Shoney's restaurant where they discussed the initial plans for the school. The men were former members of the Colonial Hills Baptist Church, and had children rising in the school system, making the need for the school they envisioned not only communally beneficial but personally paramount. They settled on a few key points: The school would not be affiliated with a church; the kids would be focused on academics, a Christian doctrine, *and* athletics; and they'd start the school backward—whereas most Christian schools began at the elementary level first, Landmark was set to be a high school first, adding elementary levels later.

The commitment to undertake the start of a school was daunting. As Bill bleakly described, "It was almost an impossible thing."

Eddie was a manager for Ryder Trucks, and Perry was a salesman for General Electric, leaving Bill as the only one of the three with any school experience. The men also knew the entire endeavor would require volunteer work, taking no money for their ongoing labor, since financial pressure served as one of their biggest challenges.

Borrowing money for the funding of the school would be necessary, but went inherently against Bill's principles, remembering his dad's notion that "you can have anything you want in life, so long as you can pay for it."

So they borrowed as little as possible and abided by Bill's "scrappy" methods, which he'd fine-tuned at his alma maters along the way.

Initially, Bill and the team purchased property that sat in a flood plain off McDonough Road in Fayetteville, Georgia. The idea was to secure cheap land, pay it off, and then use it as collateral to get a loan to construct the building. After following this plan and having a drawing of the building done by Perry Ragsdale, the group realized how long and how much it would take to build the facility. So they started to look for something temporary—starting with renting an old cabinet shop, which imposed its own host of issues.

"We'd be over there at midnight, hammering on two-by-fours," Eddie recalled.

A few days prior to the school's planned opening, the building inspector visited to check the safety code to issue a certificate of occupancy.

The inspector already didn't take too kindly to Landmark, ruing "the good athletes and good students taken from Fayette County schools."

However, his personal vendetta wouldn't be to blame for Landmark's failed inspection. The chip on his shoulder aside, the school quickly and irrefutably failed due to a lack of an air conditioner. Obtaining one would cost 10,000 dollars—an amount the founding group simply didn't have.

So the three men and their newly formed board met to pray about the situation. And, with God listening, their prayers were quickly answered. According to Eddie, "The man who rented out the warehouse to us also owned a tire company. There was a customer who came in for tires, and brought along a 10,000-dollar check. He said he'd owed the tire shop owner the money for quite some time. The owner immediately told us, 'I want to give it to you. This is not mine; God gave it to you guys.'"

Bill, Perry Duncan, and Eddie Waggoner at Shoney's restaurant, memorializing the momentous meal that sparked the creation of Landmark Christian School

With the air-conditioning problem solved, the inspector had a new one for the crew—on the Friday before the Monday that the school was scheduled to open, no less: The building required an additional exit door per the fire code. The challenge? The walls of the warehouse were composed of eight-inch-thick concrete, making the addition of a door no easy feat, even for a trio of scrappy and diligent workers. Still, as if Bill—for not the first nor last time in his life—had a straight line to talk to God, prayers were answered again; Bill happened to have worked with a contractor named Bernard while building his construction company and knew he had just the right skills to make the impossible possible. Bernard came in for the weekend job of cutting and installing the door, just in time for said door to open on Monday morning.

Prior to opening, Bill and company were met with constant criticism and doubt: "You can't do this," and "There's no way you can start a football program instantly," were two of the common sentiments. Their turnout ended up far exceeding any expectations.

Projecting around seventy-five kids for their opening year in 1989, their actual numbers more than doubled the estimate with 170 students, many recruited from local churches. The enthusiasm solidified in the minds of Bill, Eddie, and Perry that they were quenching a need of the community—and it would only go up from there.

Landmark Christian School's initial warehouse location

Mike Titus, one of the first faculty hired to teach math and coach basketball at Landmark, recalled how the turnout was particularly impressive, given the not-so-enticing exterior of the new warehouse-born venture. "Those kids were sold on the vision, not some great facilities . . . A lot of Christian schools have these dress codes and make the kids look real pretty on the outside and all. It wasn't going to be a place like that . . . We were just going to take basically average kids and give them opportunities to be successful through great programming."

When I came to Landmark, my coaching style was a lot different than Coach Thorn's. First of all, I was young, and I was foolish, and you know, all those things that come with being young. But I noticed I was really intense, and I was probably too verbal with my intensity and things. It always intrigued me . . . I never heard Coach Thorn raise his voice. I don't think I've ever heard him yell at an athlete. It just intrigued me . . . he gets asked to do things that are hard, to say the least. He never raised his voice. He'd get on them and let them know what he thought of their performance and things. But the key is . . .

I never saw him yell. I never saw him, you know, with that kind of intensity. And it really intrigued me . . . What's his secret? How's he getting what he's getting out of his kids? And to be honest, I still wonder . . . How did he do that? How did he get that out of those boys in the early days? What's the magic here that they would put up with if they worked so hard and tolerated all of that? I don't know if I have a good answer for that.

—Mike Titus, Landmark Christian Faculty

Mike's wife and future Landmark English teacher, Judy Titus, recalled her first impression of the school's facade: "I was brought up to Landmark . . . I met Bill and Patty . . . and to be honest, I didn't think I'd ever see them again because I told Mike, 'I am not working there.'" However, the vision—and the irrefutable tenacity of the ten-person faculty—kept Mike and Judy on board . . . for nearly four decades and counting.

The 1990-1991 Landmark football team senior players

Bill launched the football program—after a premature retirement party following his departure from Fayette Christian—in the same manner as he launched the school: with next to nothing. He accepted donations ("One man's trash was another man's treasure," he joked) and hand-me-downs from other public schools' old equipment, including practice dummies, used shoulder pads, and whatever they could scrounge from whoever would talk to them. At one point, Bill even drove to Georgia Southern University to speak with legendary football coach Erskine "Erk" Russell, who was a few years older than Bill when they both attended Ensley High School. Erk encouraged Bill to follow what he did when starting the football program at Georgia Southern: Do whatever he had to do and ask whomever he needed to ask to make things happen.

Landmark's initial few years were financially lean, to say the least. When the school was in need of desks, Bill began to scrounge around at local schools to see if any locations were discarding their old ones. Sure enough, Bill found some that were going to be disposed of at Fayette County High School. However, there was a catch. Due to a regulation about excess property disposal, Fayette County High School was unable to give the desks to Bill, even though they were destined for the trash. So Bill came up with his own plan. He followed the dump truck from FCHS to the county dump, and when the desks were discarded, Bill and I gathered them up, put them on a trailer towed by Bill's truck, and drove them back to Landmark. Problem solved.

—Fred Gilkeson, Landmark Christian faculty

This started with student Ben Stout's father donating a railroad car for the team to store their equipment in. Boys would drive themselves and younger teammates to the "field" (a side lot of weeds and grass behind Bill's church), change in the parking lot—or "in the trunks of their cars," according to Mike—and rinse off using the hoses postpractice. Bill would bring four orange cones to outline the unleveled field and keep the boys until the dusk or darkness forced them to stop.

Ben Stout and Coach Thorn on the field

"There were no lights, so we'd be out there in the pitch black," former quarterback Brad Waggoner recalled. However, Bill found workarounds, with some assistance. "Our parents would shine lights from their cars in the parking lot, but they didn't say anything either. They were scared of Coach Thorn."

Brad also recounted, "I don't remember a single day of high school we didn't have practice. A storm would roll in, and we'd huddle in a little room at the bottom of that church. Then, as soon as the sun came up, Coach would say, 'Well, boys, we're getting our two-hour practice in starting now.'"

Through all the late nights, long hours, grueling conditioning, and inevitable sacrifices, the boys did it all with "a special enthusiasm," according to Bill. High schoolers are certainly motivated by a competitive desire to win, an innate will to improve, and—of course—a sort of parental pressure. But above it all, the real reason they put in such work could be summed up by Brad: "You could tell Coach cared. His desk was filled with folders, full of penciled-out plans for every step of practice. I can remember being a tenth-grade quarterback, and when I'd have a bad night, Coach would pull up at my house on Saturday morning. We'd go to McCurry Park and spend hours walking through the plays. He treated you like he wanted you to succeed as a person."

At Landmark Christian School, we started where we were and used what we had. We gave the rest up to the Lord, and it was incredible.

—Fred Gilkeson, Landmark Christian faculty

Bill indeed had a knack for creating winning and devoted teams from humble beginnings, and once the Landmark football program was established, he turned his attention to wrestling: "We took out everything in the cafeteria to practice, but we didn't have a mat. In my scrounging around in the afternoons, I remembered coming in the back door at Banneker High School and seeing something that looked like the corner of a wrestling mat. It was buried in mud, but I asked the coach there, and he said, 'Come take it.' So I drove over there in my truck. It was soaked in mud, and it had a big chunk torn off, so it wasn't even a full piece. But we put it down where we'd normally eat, turned the ends up the wall, and started to wrestle."

Clint Waggoner on the cover of Bama *magazine, December 1998*

A lot of what I remember from Coach Thorn can be summed up in this: "If you'll do today what others won't . . . you'll do tomorrow what others can't." I think that is what Coach was thinking with the kids out there. Not every kid out there was going to go play for Alabama like I did. Yes, Coach Thorn was all about football, but he was also just about life and working hard and doing something that other people are not willing to do. And most people want to take the shortcut.

Most people don't want to do the hard work. They want the results. But before you get the results, you have to put in time. You have to put in effort. It's not easy. There are times when you're going to think, "I don't want to do this. Why can't I just go there and just do this?" You can, but don't expect great things if you're not willing to put in the time for it.

—Clint Waggoner, MD, Landmark Christian and University of Alabama athlete

With just a ten-person faculty, Bill took the helm of not only the football and wrestling teams, but baseball and track too. The athletes often played each sport. On top of football players being required to run track, Coach Mike Titus recalled, "We couldn't start basketball practice until after Coach Thorn quit winning football games because our basketball boys were playing football."

Baseball and track both occur during the same sports season (spring). Never one to be deterred by scheduling obstacles such as this, Bill simply held the practices back-to-back or had the athletes do two-a-day practices. As recounted by Landmark athlete Adam Hanes, "I would go to track practice in the morning, and I would run my track workout in the morning by myself. Then I would go play baseball in the afternoon. Coach said I was the only one to ever do that."

When the playoff runs would end and basketball season did start, the facilities were equally lackluster. Coach Titus claimed, "We'd wander around to find gyms to practice in." These included half-courts in Fayetteville Methodist churches, home games at Atlanta Christian College in East Point, and 6:00 a.m. and after-school practices out of Grace Christian on McDonough Road—which hosted its own set of challenges. The Grace Christian court had "dangerously slippery and dusty" concrete floors. So Coach Titus would send seniors who could drive to leave their last-period classes early to mop the concrete floor before afternoon drills could begin.

The basketball team also lacked uniforms. With fewer than a dozen jerseys for a squad of sixteen, Coach Titus recalled pairing up the bench-warming kids and allowing them to alternate games where they got to officially dress out. "I was sure

I just love the way that he breathed God into everything. He was the real deal spiritually, and that spoke volumes for those kids that were impacted by him. It wasn't just about the sports stuff. He completely immersed them in the Word all the time . . . I think that was a big deal as far as a coach, and I always respected him for that.

—Judy Titus, Landmark Christian faculty

they'd quit," Coach Titus said. "But none of them quit. They became known as the 'Hit Team.' When we'd get up in the fourth quarter, the crowd would go crazy for the hard-nosed 'Hit Team.'"

Judy Titus added, "Sometimes they'd only play for a minute . . . But they went out there like they were in the Olympics."

Being multisport athletes would end up serving the kids—and the school—well. Coach Titus recalled, "I remember when we first started playing football, we'd have fifteen boys out there on the football field, playing both ways. And I'd look and I'd see those other schools, and they'd be big, but we almost won that stinking state championship! We were always successful because you just knew our boys were going to work hard and play hard and be tough mentally."

Regarding athletics in those first years, Bill claimed, "Honestly, it should've scared a lot of people off that were looking to come to Landmark."

Outside of running miles, Coach Thorn became known for something else that also spanned miles: the length of his speeches. At one particularly memorable end-of-the-year sports banquet, Coach Thorn thought that it would be a perfect opportunity—with all his athletes and parents together—to explain to them, in detail, the development program. It lasted hours . . . spanning until 11:00 p.m. However, that was typical Coach Thorn. In his mind, his speeches were not meant to be something you liked to hear; they were meant to be something you needed to hear.

—Mike and Judy Titus, Landmark Christian faculty

The next year, a new property opportunity arose: Campbell High School, located ten miles away from their warehouse, was closing its doors. The Fairburn school was merging with Palmetto High School to become Creekside High School, leaving their current building vacant. "Then, the Lord led us to someone," Bill recalled. That "someone" was the man in charge of the Fulton County property; Bill knew him as a former student athlete at Headland and through a decade of working for Fulton County. The selling price was 250,000 dollars, which wasn't in the budget for a "scrappy" start-up like Landmark, so acquiring it required some sacrifice and lots of planning.

"We put some money down on a loan, and some of us put down collateral," said Eddie. "I had a house I had built myself that was paid for that I put up as collateral. We signed notes for the property so that if we failed, we would lose what we had. We believed in it *that* much." Mike Titus recalled the night the deal officially went down: "We were playing basketball at Flint River Academy. This was before cell phones, so Bill was on a pay phone, and we were all standing around waiting on the news. The game was over, and the facility started turning off the lights, trying to drive us out of there. But Bill stood there, talking in the pitch black. We didn't go anywhere until we found out."

Through sacrifice, some divine intervention, and one final call in a dark, empty basketball arena, the former Campbell High School property was theirs and would serve as Landmark's permanent home.

For his first ten years, Bill served as Athletic Director and dabbled in nearly every sport Landmark offered. However, after nearly forty years of chasing football state championships, Bill decided to put down the pigskin.

Landmark Christian School, Fairburn, GA

"I had a meeting with the football players and asked, 'How many of you really believe you'll do what it takes to get your body ready?'" Bill recounted. His Program was the same as it had always been, entailing daily effort, summer training, and a whole lot of running. But in 1999, the students weren't quite as willing to put in the work.

1995 Landmark football team

Some of the football parents didn't completely buy into Coach's hard work and commitment philosophy either. They wanted skill or talent to be the driving factor in how the team was coached. Bill knew his way worked, but many of the parents and the football players thought differently. "I listened to the majority and decided not to continue as football coach," Bill said, closing his thirty-two-year football coaching chapter with a record of 186-84-5, three conference championship titles, three state runner-up titles, six state playoff appearances, and three Coach of the Year accolades (in 1967, 1968, and 1991).

Bill had more than three decades of football coaching under his belt, with twenty-six years as a head coach. From his early days at Georgia Military Academy with the cadets to the Hard Labor Creek years at Headland High School, Colonial Hills days practicing on fields riddled with broken beer bottles, and winning alongside his boys from Fayette Christian, Bill had—time and time again—taken dire circumstances and created winning programs through nothing but sheer ingenuity, determination, and diligence. He'd molded thousands of lives as he instilled an unshakable sense of willpower and resiliency. And above all else, he'd spread the Gospel everywhere he went.

It is true that with some compromise or in some areas that . . . he could have stayed in place for a lot longer. I don't think he was trying to go against the administration because he just wanted this adversarial relationship. I think he was so confident in the way he was doing things. And really, I don't think he could have lived with himself if he had to compromise on his principles. I think they were so ingrained in him that he wouldn't have been happy, and he wouldn't have been successful. It's not necessarily to say his way was always the right way and the only way to do things, but for him . . . I just think it was just so ingrained in him—this, "Look, this is who I am. This is the way I got to do things. I'm not trying to be difficult, but I'm not compromising. This is how I am."

—Mike Titus, Landmark Christian Faculty

However, finishing his football coaching career was by no means the end of his coaching days. In fact, the majority of his accolades weren't even yet realized at the turn of the century. The remaining years at Landmark Christian would set the stage for some of Bill's greatest achievements and fondest memories.

Nearing age seventy, suffice it to say: Bill Thorn was just getting started.

Early Years of Landmark Coaching Recap:

10 years as Head Football Coach

Record: 64-46-1

2 regional runner-up titles

1 state runner-up title

1 State Coach of the Year Award

2 years as Head Baseball Coach

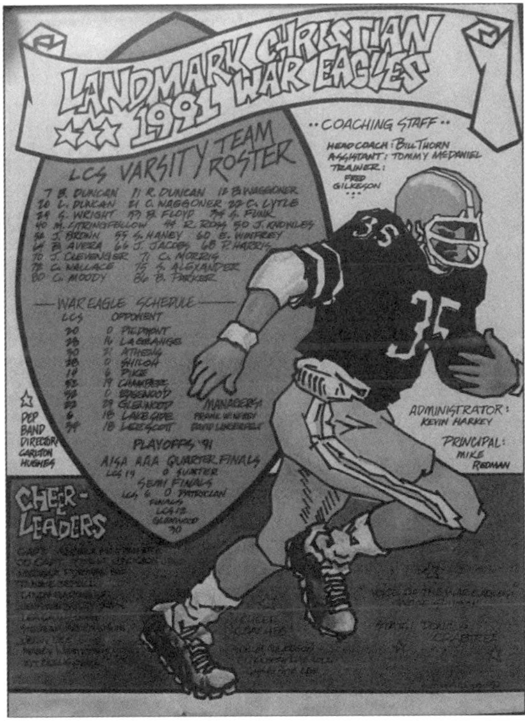

NINE

"YOU DON'T HAVE TO RUN; YOU GET TO RUN"

—PAAVO RUNNING CAMP SLOGAN

WHEN BILL ENDED HIS DAYS as a football coach, it opened the gates for him to focus on a sport that he loved and had been well accustomed to coaching for years, but with an added component. Bill's next two decades at Landmark would be largely focused on coaching track and cross-country—for boys *and girls.*

While Bill's entire career had been coaching male athletes, he was immediately impressed with his new role of coaching females as well. Bill recalled, "My first thought was, 'These girls are tough.'" Plus, he used the girls' team to recruit the boys. "I told them, 'You don't let any boy come try to woo you; put them down here with you on the track, and then we'll test them.'"

Always on the search for ways to improve athletic conditioning, Coach poses alongside the AltRed trailer.

To this day, I think that his strength program is the best in the nation. I always go back to his series of exercises because the program I did in college felt pretty elementary compared to Coach Thorn's. I don't know how he came up with it, but just all the different exercises and lifts that we were doing, I think we were top-notch. I didn't really realize that until I got to college. It made me realize how it did help so much in the running aspect, where strength played into getting faster.

—Lindy Long Jones, Landmark Christian and US Air Force Academy athlete

The Gulf Shores Thorn house, which hosted decades of spring break trips

With his focus on running, Coach ran the same Program as always—with a few new tweaks as he learned new best practices. This included muscle rolling on PVC piping, parachutes ("that blew you off the track," recalled Brad Waggoner) to rehab running injuries, a recipe for a superfood drink called "Swamp Juice" (which previous athletes described as "the most disgusting thing we'd ever drank"), creatine cocktails during meet warm-ups—and perhaps most memorably—spring break trips down to Gulf Shores.

Stemming from his real estate ventures, Bill still owned a house down in Gulf Shores, Alabama. The purpose of the trips was manifold: to continue the training "Program," to keep kids from losing progress (which would inevitably occur under alternate spring break options), and to encourage camaraderie through team dinners and bonding activities.

Despite two-a-day workouts and freezing water plunges (a Thorn-ordered treatment for lactic acid), athletes remembered the beach trips fondly.

Bill's neighbors in Gulf Shores, however, did not appreciate the spring breakers. Kids were banging weights on the concrete below the stilted houses at 7:30 a.m.—the only earlier riser at the beach being Bill himself, who would fit in a two-hour workout every single day before the sun rose, even up until eighty-eight years old—and coaches were calling out commands throughout the whole neighborhood. While one reminiscer discussed "all the crazy drills," Bill interjected with a different opinion: "They weren't crazy; they were productive."

Former Fayette Christian and Landmark Christian-athlete-turned-coach Roby Ross recalled the cold-water plunges: "I wouldn't get in there for thirty seconds up to my shins, and these eighty-pound, blue-lipped kids are getting in there twenty minutes up to their waists!"

Of course, once back at home, some things never changed: Bill's "Program" remained, logging kids' miles and times daily, and continually encouraging athletes to "do what you can." Each practice began with a two-mile run "as routine as brushing teeth." Under watchful eyes during the week, the athletes then self-recorded their weekend miles and dreaded having to report to Coach a mileage of "DNR" (Did Not Run)—or, even, to do the bare minimum. As Coach Ross recalled, "There was a certain number of required miles, and each one had a plus mark next to it. If kids only ran what was required, Coach would say, 'Did you see the plus mark? Could you have done more?' And the kid would say, 'Well, yeah, I could have.' And he'd remind them that's what the plus mark was for."

Coach enjoying a spring break workout swim in Gulf Shores

It was my first year at Landmark, and I was in Coach's house at Gulf Shores for the team trip. Every morning, you would wake up to the sound of his trampoline and him doing his morning exercises.

—Zack Truitt, Landmark Christian and University of Georgia athlete

There was no use in lying; the kids' progress—or lack thereof—would often speak for itself.

And while his Program produced some star athletes, there was no minimum requirement to reap the benefits. Long-distance runners and shotput throwers alike were coached to do their best. "Initially, they were embarrassed," Bill recalled of the 200-pound athletes running 100-meter sprints. But eventually, as they got competitive with themselves and began reaching new and unforeseen PRs, they became committed. Plus, all athletes were *strongly* encouraged to run in the 4x400 relay—the final event of every track meet.

I remember doing drills for Coach Thorn. I go back to being a seventh and eighth-grader, doing all these different plyometrics. I mean, this is like 1986 to 1987. I remember doing all these different plyometrics, and I remember thinking, "What in the world are we doing out here?" When I got to Georgia Tech, we were doing those same things. Then I find myself doing those same agility drills . . . we're still doing them today. I mean, he was a cutting-edge coach. He came up with all those things himself. It's almost sad because there are some things he came up with that I wish he could have patented back in the day.

—Brad Waggoner, Landmark Christian and Georgia Tech athlete

During the 1996 Olympic Games in Atlanta, Bill was not only a torchbearer for the games but also a scavenger! As has been the story of Bill's life, if he wanted anything, he'd find a way to pay or scrounge for it! So before the games even concluded, Bill started asking anyone who would listen, "What is going to happen to all of the track

equipment being used at these games?"

If you are persistent enough, like Bill has always been, and if you are bold enough, like Bill has always been, sometimes your persistence and boldness pay off.

Two weeks following the conclusion of the games, a slightly used, 15,000-dollar (in 1996 dollars!) world-class Olympic pole vault pit was delivered to Landmark Christian School—for free. Bill's track program had the best pole vault mat/pit in all of Georgia!

Bill also led his teams to maximize training opportunities at every twist and turn. Whether this meant pulling the team bus over into a Walmart parking lot on the way to a meet to unload hurdles and squeeze in a quick session or having kids pack jump ropes on their own family trips to use at rest stops when they couldn't easily run, his Landmark years epitomized his notion that "Winners Find a Way."

Coach Ross recalled one creative adventure the Landmark team undertook (abiding by Bill's orders) while at a track meet in Jefferson. "Coach always believed in soaking muscles to help with lactic acid between races. Well, one night, we drove our bus all around Jefferson until we found an option. There was a Holiday Inn pool that looked empty but had lights on. The gates were locked, so Coach told us to stack trash cans along the fence and climb in. I stood out as a guard, just waiting for the police to come arrest us."

> *Coach Thorn's philosophy of no excuses, hard work, dedication, and tough love spans the many years of his coaching tenure. Coach Thorn always instilled words of godly wisdom in all his runners, making us tough through the grueling workouts.*
>
> *—Lauren Toomer Moton, Landmark Christian and Georgia Southern athlete*

Of course, the dedication that Bill demanded didn't resonate with every high schooler. He had a special treatment for those who quit—and particularly for those who quit by mail. As athlete Lindy Long Jones recalled, "Some people who quit did not want to face Coach Thorn, so they'd write

Bill alongside Andrew Cathy and Dan Cathy

a letter. Coach Thorn would read each kid's letter aloud to the entire team. Nobody wanted to be embarrassed like that, so it truly instilled that quitting wasn't the answer."

However, for those who stuck to "The Program," results weren't just realized; they were inevitable. Bill described it as a flywheel sort of cycle: "The more they committed to The Program the more they succeeded. The more they succeeded, the more I wanted to push them harder. I just wanted to see them succeed."

The ninth-grade track season was coming, and I was going to run. We had a rule—it didn't matter how well you'd done all season; you didn't get your varsity letter unless you scored points at the region meet. A week before, I had a motorcycle wreck. I broke my collarbone, had a concussion, and had my tongue sewed on the inside. I knew I wasn't running. But I kept hearing Coach saying, "Winners find a way." I mustered up enough strength to pole vault, get that varsity letter, and score some points for that region meet. He taught me lots of grit and hard work that I still draw on today.

—Andrew Cathy, Landmark Christian athlete

Mehamed Gomez alongside Coach Thorn

Coach Thorn's Program was about finding out your limits and then pushing beyond that. I think a motto I still use today is, "First things first and first things right." If you don't do the first things right, all the preceding items or tasks, or whatever in your life, are not going to go properly. So I think that and the thoroughness, and really his philosophy of the way of just thinking and doing things, has stuck with me. I believe that has been a huge influence in my life. I would say it is one of the most influential up there for me.

—Mehamed Gomez, Landmark Christian and Savannah State University athlete

This notion exemplified itself in big and smaller ways. One example came in a close finish in a track meet. The way the points added up, the Landmark boys knew they needed at least a second-place finish to take home the victory. As the hurdle race came down to the finish line, Landmark's runner—Marlon Bryan—was in third place. As he approached the finish, Marlon unexpectedly plunged headfirst into the air, crossing the finish line and surpassing his competitor—and scraping off the skin of his face, chest, and arm in the process. At the state track championships that year, someone asked Bill, "How do you teach kids to dive like that?" Bill remarked, "You don't teach or make them. You get them to want to."

Bill also had a justification for his tough love: "If you think I've been hard or mean, it's just the way I grew up in Birmingham. It was a hard life. You had to put your nose to the grindstone day in and day out, just to survive . . . I applied all those principles in coaching."

And as always, Bill not only worked his athletes hard; he worked hard himself. Hannah Gravitt May recalled, "I didn't know this until I came back as a coach, but every year before the season, Coach would drive a John Deere Gator to make sure the course was ready. He would then walk a measuring wheel over the whole course so it was well marked, and the correct distance for the athletes. It was 100-plus degrees outside, and you have an

Brett Lewis with Coach Thorn, 2003

eighty-seven-year-old man humbling himself to pave the way for others to succeed."

Coach Ross echoed that notion: "You could never say he didn't care. And when someone cares about you that much, you're willing to do a lot for them."

And "a lot" they did. To nobody's great surprise, Bill's "Program" and practices—from Walmart workouts to ocean dips—led to results.

In my eighth-grade year, I ran the 200M and 400M sprints; then, my freshman year, Coach Thorn decided to put me in the hurdles. I was not too happy about that. On maybe the second or third day of practice, my brother broke his arm right in front of me. I looked at Coach Thorn and I told him, "No." But again, this man is determined. He also saw the bigger picture. Because of him seeing the bigger picture, I was able to accomplish what no one has ever accomplished before in the state of Georgia, and that was to be a sixteen-time-state championship winner—it was all because of Coach Thorn.

—Sierra Hill Dukes, Landmark Christian and Clemson University athlete

The boys' track team won the school's first Georgia state title—across any sport—in 1991, and the boys' cross-country team would take home the state title in 1999. Over the next three decades, the two teams would claim nineteen Class A championships and dominate with individual winners every year from 1995 to 2006.

Although Bill had always favored "doing your best" over strictly winning, the boys had a different mindset. On one bus trip back from a meet, the boys sat quietly, surrounded by trophies and accolades—albeit not any for first place. As the bus crossed a bridge over the Chattahoochee River, athlete Brett Lewis grabbed a trophy and spoke up: "These wouldn't be missed if we tossed them in the river. There's only one trophy, and that's for first place."

It started to sleet one day during my freshman year. Everyone was being sent home; it was kind of coming down hard and starting to stick, but [Coach Thorn] had us line up to do our run on the track. We had our layers on, and Coach said, "Nope, no layers. Just go." In that moment it seemed crazy, but . . . it set the expectations. When I went to college, if it was cold or rainy, we would revert to treadmills or cancel practice, and I would sit and think, "This is nothing to me." Stuff like that just kind of stuck with me. Even in the beginning phases of trying to get through college and that transition from high school to college, I just remember Coach reiterating, "If you've done it before, it's still there," and that stuck with me even off the track, with my art and anything I was trying to accomplish.

—Kermit Jackson, Landmark Christian and Coastal Carolina University athlete

Upon taking over the girls' teams, Bill also saw immediate results. Between track and field and cross-country, their titles amounted to eighteen, with 103 individual women's track and field and cross-country champions from 1999 to 2019.

Simply put, when you look at Bill's track and field and cross-country results at Landmark from 1991 to 2019, no other running program in Georgia state history—and perhaps even on a national level—comes close to comparison. All in all, Bill and his teams accumulated thirty-seven state championships, thirteen state runner-up titles, fifty region championships, 172 individual track and field state champions, and nine individual cross country state champions, and they accomplished a twelve-year consecutive state championship streak (from 1996 to 2008). He dominated across the board—from relays to sprints to hurdles and distance runs to field events. He coached boys and girls to equally dominant levels of success. He thrived in elevating individuals to unprecedented accomplishments while simultaneously building championship team cultures.

During the summer between my sophomore and junior years of college, I was preparing for US Air Force ROTC field training This training was intense and intimidating. The only parts I could control were my mental toughness and physical fitness. Part of my preparation included a physical fitness test, and I knew exactly who to call to help me train for the running portion—Coach! He said, "You need to get down your one-mile and 100-meter times. That's all it will take if you put in the work." Coach Thorn met me at the Landmark track that summer to coach me through exactly that.

Field training is one of the most challenging things I have endured mentally and physically. In so many moments, I couldn't help but recall Thornisms. In the summer Alabama heat, "When it's too hot for others, it's just right for us." When competing on many levels with other cadets, "Hard work given time defeats talent when talent doesn't work hard." I was so proud to call Coach at the end of that summer and let him know I made it! And not only that, but I had the highest PT overall score for all females that session—1,300-plus. I also ranked first in my flight in leadership. I attribute much of those awards to Coach Thorn.

Kaley Glenn (Cusumano), Christian Wade (McGuire), Coach Thorn, Roby Ross, and Lauren Grimsley (McGuire)

—Kaley Cusumano Glenn, Landmark Christian athlete and US Air Force Officer

However, the winning never got to Bill's head. Coach Ross recalled seeing Bill jotting notes—in his infamous, clean, cursive handwriting—in the middle of track season, penciling in rosters for the *following* year. He reminded everyone that today's victory didn't guarantee tomorrow's success and ensured he was preparing the athletes for what was coming ahead.

He didn't let the winning get to his athletes' heads either. Lindy Long Jones recalled her first open race she won: "I expected all kinds of praise. Instead, Coach simply said, 'Good job, gal.' That was it, but it did make me want to work harder and get better. Too much praise may have led to complacency."

From left to right: Andrew Cathy, Bill, Brett Lewis, and Roby Ross

Zack Truitt recalled breaking the national record for the two-mile run. Amid the celebrations with teammates, reporters herding, and crowd hoopla, Coach Thorn had just one remark: "Now, son, did you get your cool-down in on the cedar track?"

I remember those track practices where Coach just wanted us to give our all. For college, I went to the Air Force Academy to swim, and all that Coach Thorn had taught me went with me. I was never the smartest or fastest, but you better bet I could push my body and mind to the limits to never give up. Coach instilled that in me, which led me to be the best cadet and Air Force Officer that I could be. Even though he was "officially" my coach for only two years, he is the most influential coach I have ever had, and I cannot put into words how grateful I am for him. What he taught me in high school has stayed with me through my professional career, and when obstacles and hard things come up, I am able to view them as opportunities and use the mindset of "When it is too hard for others, it is just right for us."

—Lauren B. McGuire Grimsley, Landmark Christian and US Air Force Academy athlete

Bill Thorn's tenure at LCS as the track and field coach could largely be described in one word: dominance. Bill kicked things off quickly at Landmark by bringing home the boys' track team's first championship trophy shortly after opening in 1991. A few years later, the boys' team went on an incredible seven-year championship streak from 1996-2002 with three additional state championships coming in Bill's later coaching years. The girls' team was equally as impressive, with an incredible six-year championship streak from 2000-2005, with an additional state trophy in 2008.

Although all of the championship teams boasted incredible athletes and results, few teams rivaled the accomplishments of the 2004 Landmark girls' track team. In that year alone, the girls' team set four state records in the 4x100M relay, 100M hurdles, 300M hurdles, and 4x400M relay. These times still stand (as of 2025) as the fastest times ever recorded in Georgia single—A (private) state history. Along with shattering records, the 2004 Landmark girls placed in the top four finishers in twelve of the sixteen events that year. Their efforts culminated in a first place win by a staggering margin of 105 points over second-place Jenkins County. This commanding win was only eclipsed by their previous year's 127-point win over Jefferson.

Bill, alongside fellow coaches Roby Ross and Andrew Cathy, with the 2004 Landmark girls' track team. Team members were: Ciara Willis, Jessica Vautin, Janell Henderson, Ebonne Holyfield, Evette Holyfield, Sarah King, Lynette Fitts, Heather Hayes, Kristina Eden, and Sierra Hill.

Along with his triple-digit victories over the second-place teams, Bill's athletes were frequently atop the podium in their respective events. After his first athlete, Mark Brown, topped the podium in 1969 after winning the 1600M run, Bill went on to coach an additional 163 Landmark athletes to the top spot. Bill's intensive training program

Nicole Fegans, 2014

yielded results across nearly every track and field event, as he coached athletes to victory in 15 of the 16 track events over the course of his career. His efforts and subsequent success earned him track and field "Coach of the Year" awards by several different organizations a record-setting 64 times.

Largely due to this inimitable focus and dogged adherence to the systems—cool-downs and all—Bill's runners were absolutely dominant. However, Bill never attributed it entirely to "The Program": "You can have everything going for you. You can have a program you know that works because it's been proven. You can know everything about your sport. But when it gets down to the very core of any kind of success, you've got nothing unless you can get the kids to do it!"

And this was the reason no competitors could ever seem to replicate Landmark's success. Marietta High School coach Roscoe Googe said that the two-mile warm-up alone would cause him to "lose his whole team." Coach Scott Neal from Tallulah Falls echoed the impressiveness, telling Bill, "Y'all always have great performances at State," to which Bill reminded him, "It's not by accident; it's designed that way." Bill even offered to put on clinics for other coaches and athletes, to share his "Program" with anyone who would listen. "But as soon as I told them what I did, they'd say, 'That'll never work in my school; the kids will never do it.'"

The last clinic we worked together in was in 2020. He said, "Marsh, all I want to be is a difference maker." Do you hear that? "All I want to be is a difference maker." It's quiet. It's private. It doesn't need all the accolades. And the big thing is: It's not fancy. It's hard work, blood, sweat, tears, and commitment.

—Marshall Sellers, Paavo Running Camps

I'm the only one who knows if I really did my best today. I think it's a lot of self-accountability that [Coach Thorn] rubs into you that you don't realize until it's four years later, and you're done with "The Program." You're like, "Wow, that kind of taught me to push through harder when I thought I couldn't."

—Nicole Fegans, Landmark Christian and Georgia Tech athlete

This sentiment was never truer than in one example at a track meet at Marist High School. The skies opened up when the meet was scheduled to get underway, unleashing torrential downpours and ripples of thunder. The start time was repeatedly delayed until, eventually, the meet was altogether canceled. Teams trickled away at the cancellation announcement just as the skies began to clear; Bill's team, of course, had waited out the storm. And when the other teams were long gone—including the host school's team and staff—Bill's entire team ran their 4x400 relays.

So what exactly encouraged a bunch of teenagers to devote themselves the way Bill's athletes did, year after year after year?

First and foremost: respect. Bill would run just as the kids did, as he coached through his sixties, seventies, and eighties. "It's helpful for them to see that if I can do it at my age, they can do it at theirs," Bill stated.

However, age wasn't the only hurdle Bill faced during his Landmark years. Within his first decade at the school, he would be presented with an additional battle. During an annual physical

While renovating an old building at Landmark in 2012, we ran across a large room that was eventually going to be torn down. The space was filled with old junk and 250-plus forgotten (non-state-championship) trophies. Most of the trophies were covered in mold from the leaking roof. There were just too many trophies to keep on display at the school gym, so hundreds had been stored away. So many trophies that kept piling up from years and years of success.

—Chuck Cusumano, parent of three Landmark Christian athletes

in the mid-'90s, Bill's doctor felt lumps on his prostate.

Incidences of prostate cancer were severely on the rise, with a more than 50 percent increase between the late '80s and early '90s. However, these numbers were largely due to improved testing technology with the introduction of prostate-specific antigen (PSA) blood tests.

Bill would undergo this PSA test, scoring a four (compared to a zero, which would've indicated he was cancer-free).

"There weren't 'phases,' and they didn't know much about it back then . . . just that it was deadly," Bill said. "But I wanted to live as long as I could. That's the competitiveness in me. So I got deeply involved in finding out as much as I could about the disease."

While incidences were on the rise and while it *was* deadly, mortality rates were on the decline—thanks, in large part, to earlier diagnoses and a plethora of treatment options . . . many of which Bill declined.

"They'd say, 'You've got to do something.' But 'doing something' entailed having your prostate removed," Bill recalled, which wasn't his first-choice solution. "It would be messy; they'd go in and make a big incision from your belly button down. But then I asked the real big question: 'If I remove the prostate, is that it? Nothing comes back?' And they couldn't positively answer that."

Bill also didn't like the prospect of radiation in his body, nor the alternative concept of cryotherapy. So instead, he relied on the same protocols that had served him well for more than sixty years: prayer and nourishing and supplementing his God-given body naturally. He began boosting his immune system through diet and vitamins—and a whole lot of grapefruit juice.

A coach's biggest test

Diagnosed with cancer, Landmark Christain's Bill Thorn challenges h[illegible] athletes and himself

Newspaper article detailing Bill's cancer fight, August 1998

Throughout his battle, Bill wasn't deterred or angered: "Cancer is just something we all have here with us," he told a local newspaper. "I'm just thankful to know I have it, so I can do something about it . . . It's in the Lord's hands, so I don't really worry about it."

Bill began seeing urologists regularly to monitor his PSA readings. "I never did get down to zero," Bill stated, nearly thirty years after his initial diagnosis. "But neither do those people who went through surgery!"

His doctors agreed. His primary urologist, Dr. Scott Shelfo, a young doctor and 1991 graduate from Albany Medical College, had just one piece of advice for Bill: "Keep doing whatever you're doing." Bill recalled, "He told me, 'You're my hero. Whatever you're doing, I want to be like you.'"

In addition to earning respect by doing everything he expected his athletes to do, Bill also walked the talk by living out a "team-first" mentality, even if no one ostensibly knew it. One example came when he accepted the position of Athletic Director at Landmark and was given a 2,000-dollar raise—a hefty increase in those days. "I started thinking of the other coaches, and they weren't going to receive any kind of increase. So I divided it up among the five coaches, because they certainly deserved it."

Coach Thorn has had a huge impact on our entire family. Our daughter, Turner, was a soccer player until she broke her arm in the spring of her fifth-grade year. She had to stop playing and was terribly bored coming home from school every afternoon. She asked Coach Ross if she could have a job timing the Landmark track team. This started her acquaintance with Coach Thorn.

Coach Thorn and Turner Guerard

After spending the spring helping out, she came home and announced that she was no longer interested in soccer, but instead, wanted to run for Coach Thorn. Her dad and I were not so sure about this decision—we knew that timing the team would be quite different than running with the team. But Turner has never been easily deterred once her mind is made up, and so she went out for cross country in the fall of her sixth-grade year. Coach Thorn did not really distinguish between a sixth-grader or a twelfth-grader on his team—all would work hard under his Program, and much was expected of them. This thrilled Turner, and she thrived under his coaching.

Coach Thorn was tough, but our kids knew they were loved by him. Turner understood this and wanted to give her best and make him proud. She had the privilege of running under his leadership for several years, and the lessons she learned (and we all learned) have probably made the most impact on her of any teacher or coach.

When Coach Thorn retired, we wanted to be intentional about spending time with him and Patty. So several families and ours started having once-a-month dinners at their home. We plan a date, bring supper, and spend time together, sharing and listening to old stories. Coach doesn't forget an athlete or a detail about the races he's watched over the years. It is truly amazing! They continue to model godliness, obedience, consistency, love, and truth to our children and family. We would not trade a minute of time we have spent with them on their back porch or around the dining room table.

—Alison Guerard, parent of Landmark Christian athlete

Mike Titus recalled Coach's quiet devotion to building Landmark—literally. "The same relentlessness that he put into sports, he put into Landmark. There was never a workday that I came to that he and Patty weren't there doing something. He'd be in the showers, quietly scraping away with a putty knife. He wouldn't make a big announcement; he'd just go off in the corner and do his thing. People knew he was committed to sports, but I don't think people saw how committed he was to the school as well."

Another factor that contributed to his kids buying into "The Program" came down to Bill's ridiculous and ruthless consistency. As one Landmark parent noted, "For a lot of kids, that consistency was a form of love, because they finally had something they knew they could count on."

Plus, the athletes inevitably became somewhat addicted to success—even if that meant sacrifice. Lindy Long Jones recalled, "High school prom was two days before a regional meet. Coach didn't want students out late, so a chaperone—who just so happened to be my date's mom—brought me home hours before the end of the night . . . without my date. But without making sacrifices, I don't think I would have been able to run in college, or ever get to the level I wanted to."

Upon reflecting on his Landmark athletes, Bill had one overwhelming sentiment: "Sometimes it looked impossible, yet they didn't give up. They kept on going."

Through some combination of respect, sacrifice, dedication, devotion, nutrition, rest and recovery, and perhaps a bit of Swamp Juice, overcoming the impossible became achievable—much like the start of Landmark itself, a once "almost impossible thing."

And much like his athletes, Bill wasn't going to give up either. Upon his retirement from Landmark at age eighty-eight, he would keep going and further his legacy in yet another arena: the Peachtree Road Race.

I homeschooled my kids for fifteen years; I looked long and hard around Atlanta to find the right place to take them after those years at home. They were athletic. I knew I wanted high academics, athletics, and fine arts. Landmark was the only place I could find that met all those requirements of working toward excellence in those fields. But we spent years with our kids being athletes at home during homeschool because they could do a lot of events. But soccer had been my oldest daughter, Christian's, main sport.

So we got to Landmark. Both my girls—Lauren and Christian—got there first in eighth and ninth grade and played basketball as well as swimming. Well, spring is rolling around, and Christian comes home, and it's finally soccer season. It's finally what we're good at. And she comes home and goes, "Mom, I think I want to run track this year." I'm like, "What are you talking about? It's soccer season."

She goes, "I just think I want to try track. That's what all my friends are doing." I told her, "We spent all this money. Let's just pray about this for a little while. Let's just make sure this is what you're supposed to do."

In the meantime (back in 2004/2005), a roast of Coach Thorn was being held to raise money to resurface the track. Somebody invited us to go . . . I didn't know anything about anybody at Landmark, as this was our first year at the school. I sat there for four hours and listened to athletes from the '50s, '60s, '70s, and '80s talk about what that man had done in their lives. I was just in awe.

So I'm driving home that night after the banquet, and I'm thinking, "You know, Christian, I think it might be a good idea for you to run track this year." It was the best decision I ever made. And then I got home, and I looked at my other three kids and said, "You're all running for Coach Thorn. I don't care if you like running. I don't care if you hate running. You're all running for Coach Thorn."

—Lauren R. McGuire, Chick-fil-A Operator and parent of four Landmark Christian athletes

Landmark Coaching Recap:

30 years as Boys' Head Track Coach
11 state championships
50 first-place event wins at state meets (individual state-championship athletes)
6 state runner-up titles
18 region championships
19x Boys' Track Regional Coach of the Year
10x Boys' Track State Coach of the Year
10x Atlanta Track Club Coach of the Year
2x National Sectional Boys' Coach of the Year
1x National Boys' Track Coach of the Year

20 years as Girls' Head Track Coach
7 state championships
60 first-place event wins at state meets (individual state championship athletes)
3 state runner-up titles
9 regional championships
9x Regional Girls' Track Coach of the Year
7x Atlanta Track Club Coach of the Year
7x Girls' State Coach of the Year

20 years as Boys' Cross-Country Head Coach
7 state championships
4 state runner-up titles
9 regional championships
10x Regional Boys' Cross-Country Coach of the Year
8x Atlanta Track Club Boys' Cross-Country Coach of the Year
8x State Boys' Cross-Country Coach of the Year

20 years as Girls' Cross-Country Head Coach
10 state championships

1 state runner-up title
13 regional championships
13x Girls' Cross-Country Regional Coach of the Year
11x Atlanta Track Club Girls' Cross-Country Coach of the Year
10x State Girls' Cross-Country Coach of the Year

Bill and Coach Roby Ross at Landmark Christian School

COACH THORN'S PAAVO/ PACE-PER-MILE (PPM) PROGRAM

BACKGROUND

IN 1997, IN WHAT COULD BEST BE DESCRIBED as an act of divine intervention in Bill's life, a flyer advertising a Paavo Coaching Clinic in Illinois found its way into the Thorn family's mailbox. Intrigued by the ad but wanting more details before making the trip from Georgia, Coach Thorn called the number on the flyer and flatly asked the person who picked up the phone, "I just got your clinic flyer . . . Tell me one good reason why I should come all the way up to Chicago for your clinic?"

Lucky for Coach Thorn (and the hundreds of athletes that Bill would have the opportunity of teaching over the next couple of decades), Marshall Sellers was the person on the other end of the line and wasn't deterred by the abrupt start to the conversation. "If you want an exactness of training to convert an exactness in racing results, and if you want to work hard at the coaching process to get runners to do that, and if you want the most total and inclusive process out there, then that will be what you will get at the clinic," Sellers bluntly replied.

Sold at the direct and no-nonsense response, Bill simply replied, "Okay, I'll see if I can get a flight to Chicago."

Bill, at age sixty-seven, was the first one to check in at the clinic and took a seat in the front row, center seat. With a recorder, stack of blank cassette tapes, and notebook, Bill listened with an intensity no other participant showed. At the end of the clinic, Bill went up to Sellers and extended his hand. "I have been looking for this my entire life," Bill said.

The rest, as they say, is history.

Bill and Marshall would go on to host numerous Paavo Clinics together, with several held at the Landmark campus. Bill would mold the Paavo program into his own unique blend of Paavo principles and Thornisms to create a winning recipe with incredible results. Dozens of individual state champions, along with dozens of team state championships, would blossom from the seeds of knowledge gleaned from the initial Paavo clinic, with many Coach Thorn-taught athletes carrying those same principles into their own winning coaching careers.

THE DETAILS OF THE PAAVO/PACE-PER-MILE

Designed to strategically and incrementally increase an athlete's speed and distance abilities, the Pace-Per-Mile (PPM) Program requires an athlete to run a specific number of miles at an expected pace over the course of one week. The Paavo Training System (named after 1920s running legend Paavo Nurmi) and PPM are often used interchangeably, with implementation style at the discretion of the individual coach.

Although the PPM Program was initially designed for cross-country runners, Coach Thorn was possibly the first coach to implement "The Program" for sprinters, with incredible results.

How the PPM Program Works

The PPM program runs in one-week training cycles, with each plan specifically tailored to the individual athlete's capabilities and goals. Each day within the one-week cycle requires the athlete to complete a training run with mileage and/or speed requirements. If the athlete completes all daily runs at the specified mileage and pace, they "earn" the right to gradually increase their mileage and/or speed requirements for the following week.

Weekly Training Regimen:

- **Monday*:** Always a long run; no pace requirements.
- **Tuesday:** Shortest, fastest day. All out, as fast as possible.
- **Wednesday:** Recovery run; time is based on Tuesday's average, so

*While the start date of "The Program" is up to the coach or athlete, most Programs start on Monday.

it's a bit longer and slower than the previous day.

- **Thursday:** Toughest run of the week; duplicates Tuesday's run in the exact time or faster, followed by additional distance (usually a mile or so, as fast as possible).
- **Friday:** Recovery run; time is based on Thursday's average, so it's a bit longer and slower than the previous day.
- **Saturday:** During the season, this is usually meet day. Offseason means this is a long-run day. This is the run where you'll do your most mileage at a time for the week. Then, one of those miles is another all-out racing mile.
- **Sunday:** Recovery run.

Key Terms and Abbreviations for the PPM Program:

- **LR:** Long Run
- **SPPM:** Short Pace Per Mile. This is an "all-out pace," run as fast as a runner can possibly go over a comparatively shorter distance to LPPM.
- **LPPM:** Long Pace Per Mile. This requires the athlete to run the same distances as the previous SPPM at the same time or faster, with the additional distance as fast as the runner can manage.
- **CT:** Critical Threshold. This is used as part of an athlete's recovery days; the runner completes each mile by adding forty-five seconds to the previous PPM average.
- **TM:** Timed Mile (or a timed run of the distance you're training for).
- **LD:** Long Day. This is the total mileage completed within the day, but it does not have to be run all at once.
- **HLT:** High-Level Training. Offseason meet simulation. During the offseason, this is used to prepare the athlete for the physical load they experience during a typical meet day. Comprised of warm-up one mile, all-out one-mile, cool-down 800m, all-out 800m, cool-down 800m, all-out 400m, and cool-down one mile.
- **SI:** Short Intervals. After completing a long PPM run of six to nine miles, a runner is eligible to move into the pure speed portion of "The Program." This includes track workouts of speed SIs and PIs.

- **PI:** Pace Intervals. Short, intense runs at a certain pace over a specified distance.

PPM Program Example Training Schedules

SPRINTER PPM PROGRAM SAMPLE SCHEDULE (MALE AND FEMALE)								
MILES	MON	TUE	WED	THUR	FRI	SAT	SUN	WEEK'S INFORMATION
Per Week	LR	SPPM	CT	LPPM	CT	TM/ LD	CT	
10	1	1	1	1	1	1	1	Tues, Thurs, and Sat, 800 warm-up and cool-down
13	1	1	1	1	1	1	1	Tues, Thurs, and Sat, 1-mile warm-up and cool-down
16	2	1	1	2	2	1	2	Tues, Thurs, and Sat, 1-mile warm-up and cool-down
18	2	1	2	2	2	1	2	Tues, Thurs, and Sat, 1-mile warm-up and cool-down
20	3	1	2	2	2	1	2	Tues, Thurs, and Sat, 1-mile warm-up and cool-down, plus an additional mile
23	3	1	3	2	3	1	3	Tues, Thurs, and Sat, 1-mile warm-up and cool-down, plus an additional mile

MALE DISTANCE PPM PROGRAM SAMPLE SCHEDULE								
MILES	MON	TUE	WED	THUR	FRI	SAT	SUN	WEEK'S INFORMATION
Per Week	LR	SPPM	CT	LPPM	CT	TM/ LD	CT	
20	4	1	2	3	2	1+5	3	Tues and Thurs, 1-mile warm-up and cool-down
30	6	2	5	4	4	1+7	4	Tues and Thurs, 1-mile warm-up and cool-down
40	8	3	6	5	5	1+9	6	Tues and Thurs, 1-mile warm-up and cool-down
50	9	4	8	6	7	1+10	6	Tues and Thurs, 1-mile warm-up and cool-down

FEMALE DISTANCE PPM PROGRAM SAMPLE SCHEDULE								
MILES	MON	TUE	WED	THUR	FRI	SAT	SUN	WEEK'S INFORMATION
Per Week	LR	SPPM	CT	LPPM	CT	TM/ LD	CT	
21	3	2	3	3	2	1+4	3	Tues and Thurs, 1-mile warm-up and cool-down
28	5	3	4	4	3	1+6	4	Tues and Thurs, 1-mile warm-up and cool-down
35	6	4	5	5	4	1+7	5	Tues and Thurs, 1-mile warm-up and cool-down

SHORT INTERVAL (SI)/PACE INTERVAL (PI) SAMPLE SCHEDULE					
Week	MONDAY	TUESDAY	WEDNESDAY	THURSDAY	FRIDAY
1	Low 5-6x400m 2x100m (All Out)	CT	CT	High 9-10x400m	CT
2	Low 1x100m 1x200m	CT	High	CT	Low
3	High	CT	CT	Low	CT
4	High	Low PIs 5x200 (All Out)	CT	CT	Low
5	High	High PIs 10x200 2x200 (All Out)	CT	CT	Low

TEN

"WHEN IT'S HARD TO RUN, RUN HARD"

—PAAVO RUNNING CAMP SLOGAN

FOR THOSE WHO KNOW BILL BEST, it's understood that his no-nonsense, gritty attitude doesn't begin and end with coaching. Stern stubbornness and unrelenting dedication are elements of his mindset—a perspective that not only garnered him success in life but had a ripple effect on the thousands of other lives he touched.

And for Bill, that unwavering commitment is most obvious in more than just one specific aspect of his life: It comes through his coaching, his dedication to his relationship with Jesus, and his determination to share the Gospel.

Still, for those looking to understand the overarching theme of Bill's character, his commitment, and who he truly is at his core, they need only look to one example to see a neat and tidy illustration of it all: the Peachtree Road Race.

For fifty-three years, there were a few things you could guarantee on every Fourth of July in Atlanta: sweltering humidity, red-white-and-blue-clad patrons shoulder-to-sweaty-shoulder on the Metropolitan Atlanta Rapid Transit Authority (MARTA), and Coach Bill Thorn at the starting line of the Peachtree.

AJC Peachtree Road Race advertisement

Bill, Bill Jr., and Terry (center) along with the original 150 participants at the starting line of the inaugural 1970 Peachtree Road Race. 110 of the participants would finish the race and become known as the "original 110."

Although now touted as the "world's largest 10K" with 60,000 annual participants (a cap that has steadily risen over the years), the race had humble beginnings in 1970. The first year, 150 participants shared the streets with Atlanta holiday traffic, running from the old Sears parking lot on the corner of Peachtree and Roswell Road and finishing at Central City Park—for the 110 that managed to finish, that is. It took until 1971 for the now-famous Peachtree T-shirts to be handed out at the end of the 6.2 miles, and until 1978 for the race to reconfigure its route to end in the heart of iconic Piedmont Park.

Bill at his 50th Peachtree Road Race

More than five decades later, the Independence Day 10K is world-renowned, attracting top runners from around the globe to brave it out for the Peachtree Cup—or to simply survive Cardiac Hill and enjoy the hundreds of thousands of cheering onlookers lining Peachtree Street from Buckhead to Midtown. Although the route is considered a festivity—with music consistently blasting, patriotic spirits high, and plenty of drinks, doughnuts, and even a sprinkling of "holy water" outside of The Cathedral of St. Philip at Mile Two—it's no easy feat. Mile Three begins the infamous "Cardiac Hill," an almost-mile uphill climb in which the course rises more than twelve stories; add in the reliable Georgia heat and the other numerous Atlanta hills that haven't yet earned their own monikers, and any Peachtree finisher knows their T-shirt prize is well earned and worn with pride.

For the man who has fifty-three of them (and nearly as many pairs of the official "race day shoes" collected and stowed away in his room of running accolades), the Peachtree wasn't just a tradition; it was a lifestyle. It was the culmination of his lifelong commitment to health and fitness, a testament to his tenacity, and proof that his Thornisms were not just taught; they were lived. Every moment he'd pushed his runners or football players to run faster, run harder, or choose the extra mile even when they didn't want to, he was doing the same.

In the late '80s, my brothers Rob and Rick Ross played for Coach Thorn at Landmark. Because of my passion for my brothers and for football, I would spend my days watching them practice and would stand on the sidelines. One thing to know about Coach Thorn is that he will put anybody to work. So with my clipboard, paper, and pencils, I joined his team by keeping his football stats.

I've personally run about thirty Peachtree Road Races, but his commitment to his health and determination to run every year is inspiring. I'm thirty years younger, and he outran me every time. I would always enjoy visiting him and seeing every Peachtree Road Race T-shirt he had hanging in his garage. No doubt he would always take home a medal in his division. He is one of the most hardworking and disciplined men of God I've ever known.

—Donald Crabtree, Landmark Christian football stat keeper

Of course, "Bill Thorn" was already a name well known by the Atlanta Track Club, which puts on the Peachtree and whose primary purpose of forming in the '60s was to honor the best track athletes in the state. Throughout Bill's coaching tenure, the club awarded him Coach of the Year honors fifty-three times and enshrined him in their Hall of Fame. However, coaching achievements aside, Bill would ensure his name was instilled in their history books for another reason.

In the words of Rich Kenah, Executive Director of the Atlanta Track Club, "It seems so appropriate that one of the most accomplished coaches in state history is the one person who has had the mental focus, physical stamina, and emotional commitment to find the Peachtree finish line each and every year."

Even the "Peachtree 50" website, celebrating its fiftieth anniversary in 2019, noted, "The great Johnny Kelley, who completed the Boston Marathon 58 times from 1928-1992 and in 2000 was named "Runner of the Century" by Runner's World magazine, missed a year—1968, after hernia surgery."

However, the road to becoming the "only man who had run every Peachtree" wasn't always easy, or even intentional.

"All I know is that none of this was ever planned from the beginning," Bill related of his accolade that prompted Atlanta Track Club's Janet Monk to nickname him "our Ironman of the Peachtree."

Although Bill had played sports all his young, adult life, he didn't begin running until his late thirties, when he picked up Dr. Kenneth Cooper's book *Aerobics*.

Dan and Bill at Peachtree Road Races through the decades

Prior to Bill's 49th Peachtree, Dan Cathy wrote: "Bill Thorn, my son Andrew's high school coach, and our collective mentor, continues to inspire me."

—Dan T. Cathy, Chairman, Chick-fil-A

Dr. Cooper was an Air Force physician who outlined what he called "the most effective physical fitness plan ever for men and women"—and it was simple. It offered a point system for various physical activities. Bill aimed for thirty points per week, initially, which could be accomplished by running one mile per day, Mondays through Fridays.

At the time he began running, he was coaching at Headland High School in the late 1950s. During the week, he'd go for a run between classes and enjoyed his weekends off. However, when he found it particularly difficult to restart his routine come Monday, he began looking for opportunities to run on the weekends. That's when he discovered road races, as well as a small but passionate crowd of other runners, including Tim Singleton, a standout athlete at Druid Hills High School, who would go on to be a star athlete at Georgia Tech and the soon-to-be founding father of the inaugural Peachtree Road Race.

Soon, Bill was chasing more miles than points, and Tim told him about a little Fourth of July event he was starting up. Bill showed up at the starting line with both of his sons, then ages ten and six, by his side as part of the 150 original participants of the race.

Cover of Aerobics

"They didn't have to run; they got to run," Bill would later recount in regard to bringing his young boys along. They—along with the "original 110" (the number of original participants who finished the inaugural run) ran that first race, never predicting it would become a long-standing tradition and an enormously popular road race, growing by the year. What soon became a massive event with tens of thousands of participants started as a "family-type" situation at the beginning. And Bill was there for every year of its growth.

Friend, pastor, and fellow runner Howard Dial was inspired by Bill's Peachtree. "When I met Bill at a Bible study around 1970, Bill had just run his first Peachtree, and I'd never run six miles in my life," Howard said. He attempted to jog, but his "deck shoes" resulted in horrible shin splints. "Bill took me out and bought me a brand-new pair of Adidas. I thought I was running on clouds."

In 2019, I was part of the world-class athlete program for the United States Air Force. It was my first chance to run semiprofessionally at the Peachtree Road Race . . . to run as an elite. I was so excited to go back to my hometown for the first time since high school and run. The Atlanta Track Club was hosting elite runners from around the world for a dinner at an Atlanta hotel ballroom downtown, and Coach Thorn was the main speaker. I received an invitation to attend, and when Coach Thorn stood up to speak, he pointed to me and said, "This athlete ran for me at Landmark Christian, and she's going to the Olympics." I did make it through to eventually run at the Olympic trials, also in Atlanta. However, in November, before the trials in February, my dad passed away. I wanted to quit, as grief was consuming all of my energy. But I leaned on lessons from Coach Thorn to get me through it. Going through the adversity of running teaches you about life. He taught me with hard work and trusting God, you really can overcome anything.

—Lindy Long Jones, Landmark Christian
and US Air Force Academy athlete

Howard signed up for his first Peachtree in 1972 and has run every one since—many by Bill's side. There were highs—such as when Bill finally broke forty minutes despite crowds almost blocking his path two blocks from the finish line. As Bill recalled, "It was my best time because it was the day that I planned to have my best time," his signature mindset shining through.

However, there were certainly lows throughout fifty-three years of running as well.

"During Bill's cancer diagnosis, he was having a tough time, passing blood and fighting a little problem of self-doubt," Howard remembered of one of their mid-'90s races. Bill became the only man to run every Peachtree in 1993 (despite a badly sprained ankle that year) after the only other man to have done so—Don Gamel—had to sit out the race with arthritis in his knee. However, even a cancer battle wasn't going to keep Bill from the hills and humidity of Atlanta. As Howard recalled, "We talked the whole way about how we would run when we got really old."

Bill encouraged his sons to pursue running from a young age. When the Greenbriar Mall opened in Atlanta in 1965, Bill got an idea. He mapped out an 800m course on the inside of the mall and would take Bill Jr. and Terry before school each morning at 6:00 a.m. to run four to eight miles while the shopkeepers prepared their stores for daily opening.

Like most things in Bill Thorn's life, if something momentous was happening in the sports arena, he was there. Such is the story of Bill's selection and participation in the Olympic Torch Relay.

First used at the 1936 Berlin Summer Games, the modern torches of the Winter and Summer Games are designed to resist the effects of wind and rain as the torch relay starts its journey from Olympia, Greece, where it is lit from the sun's rays with a parabolic mirror to ignite the Olympic flame. The flame is then relayed to the host city for the lighting of the official start of the respective Games.

In 1996, when Atlanta hosted the Summer Olympic Games, Bill and his brother were both relay runners on the iconic trek of the Flame. Proudly carrying the torch through the streets of

Atlanta, the trek concluded with the momentous lighting of the cauldron by Muhammad Ali (the 1960 gold medalist in boxing) as he battled the effects of Parkinson's disease.

In 2004, Bill was again selected as an official Olympic torchbearer as the flame made a historic relay around the globe for the first time in Olympic history.

Leave it to Bill to hold true to that plan. After all, he'd lived his life without knowing how to quit. "If your body is pushed, you'll pass out. The Lord gave you the mechanisms to handle that. You're not going to kill yourself. So you just run and never quit." This was also the advice he'd passed down to his players over the years: that sweat and hard work were things that you could get through and that you could push through being uncomfortable to get results. He was never just saying those things to his players or runners—he was experiencing them firsthand by living them himself.

Even when the race went virtual and took place on Thanksgiving in 2020, Bill showed up (on both July Fourth—for tradition's sake—and again in November) at the starting line of a predetermined, 6.2-mile route he'd meticulously mapped out around a lake in his Tyrone, Georgia, neighborhood. "The first mile was going well," Howard recalled of the November run, but by the end, Bill's legs began faltering. After nearly four hours and struggling toward the finish line with Howard under one shoulder and close neighbor Mitch Breggerman encouraging him to finish, eighty-nine-year-old Bill, Howard, and Mitch all crossed the finish line together for Bill's fifty-first Peachtree.

Two years later, at age ninety-one and coming upon Peachtree number fifty-three, Bill's training forecasted a questionable and formidable outlook. He'd maintained his standard workout regimen over the years—from running laps before football games to waking up at 6:00 a.m. for a two-hour workout before the Gulf Shores practices began. Postretirement, his routine continued—which included ninety daily minutes (and a rest day of only half of the disciplined routine on Sundays) of strength and cardio training, mixing up weights, push-ups, bouncing on his cherished trampoline, stretching, running, walking, and core work—but a fall while out walking in the streets of his subdivision had left him bloody, and an ankle injury had left him limping.

"I don't know how to quit," Bill repeated in June, leading up to the big day, alternating his swollen ankle between dunks in ice baths and bouts of hot water treatment.

However, for Bill, completing Peachtrees was never about the recognition. It was about the journey: "You just do one, and you don't stop. You put one foot in front of the other and keep going."

So like he always had—in coaching, in running, and in life—he powered on. He made it to the startling line of the fifty-third Peachtree, injured ankle and all. With a limp that led him toward the gutters, Bill toughed out the 6.2 miles, and—when he made it to the finish tape three-and-a-half hours later—his own fan section was there, along with a Tyrone policeman, to cheer him to the finish line.

He'd completed his fifty-third and final Peachtree.

In 2023, Bill made the momentous decision to hang up his running shoes and tie a bow on his Peachtree story. After riding the race in a pace car as the Grand Marshal, Bill crossed the finish line on foot one final time. And something else special happened: Bill's name was engraved on the Peachtree Road Race Champion's Cup and stands as the only name on the cup who isn't an actual race winner.

I can't begin to imagine what it would be like to run the same race every year for fifty years. Bill Thorn is absolutely incredible! Staying motivated year in and year out is one thing, but keeping your body healthy enough to race every single year is even more amazing than never having anything go wrong. That kind of consistent dedication is so inspiring. Maybe he can share some of his secrets with me.

—Amy Cragg, two-time Olympian, 2017 IAAF World Championships marathon bronze medalist, and the 2014 AJC Peachtree Road Race champion

Bill's Peachtree legend is a beautiful illustration of his life, tied up in a neat little package, showing an overarching view of who he is as a person. So many people view Bill's success in running fifty-three Peachtrees as winning—stepping up to that starting line despite unforeseen obstacles, health issues, and the natural aging process. But Bill never cared about winning—not even when he coached all those years. Winning was a fringe benefit, a brushstroke in the bigger picture of it all.

He is scrappy. He is relentless. He is inspiring. But above all, he is tireless in his pursuit to show the world what matters most: a focus on the Lord, a good disposition, and an unshakable mindset.

Mike Mitchell, Bill's former Headland quarterback, looked on as Bill crossed that finish line for the fifty-third Peachtree race, watching his old coach smiling for photos as he stood on his wobbly ankle.

As a kid, Mike had trudged alongside his coach for what felt like hundreds of miles in preparation for the football season—running until he couldn't, dragging his feet when they felt heavy, pushing himself further for a man whom he couldn't bear to let down. What he couldn't have understood then is that he was really stepping one foot in front of the other, putting in the work to become the man he is today.

He didn't have to know it at the time; it was something his coach knew all along.

Now, as an adult, he'd run alongside his coach in what would be his last Peachtree race—a beautiful ending to a piece of his legacy.

"You know," Mike said, thinking back on his Headland days, "we call ourselves 'The Briar Boys' . . . There's no better way to describe Coach. He's Thorn, and I think it's a good name for him. After all, you don't mess with the briar."

1 Corinthians 9:24-27 (ERV)

You know that in a race all the runners run, but only one runner gets the prize. So run like that. Run to win! All who compete in the games use strict training. They do this so that they can win a prize—one that doesn't last. But our prize is one that will last forever. So I run like someone who has a goal. I fight like a boxer who is hitting something, not just the air. It is my own body. I fight to make it do what I want. I do this so that I won't miss getting the prize myself after telling others about it.

Bill and sons prior to the 1972 Peachtree Road Race

Bill with pastor and friend Howard Dial at the 2000 Peachtree Road Race

Bill and daughter Cheryl at the 2009 Peachtree Road Race

Bill with granddaughter Kenzie Bayman at Bill's 44th Peachtree Road Race

Bill at the 2016 Peachtree Road Race

Bill at the finish line of his 50th Peachtree Road Race

Bill at the finish line of his 53rd Peachtree Road Race in 2023 (photo courtesy of The Atlanta Journal-Constitution*)*

Cheryl Thorn Thrasher in front of a signature panel hosted by the AJC Peachtree Road Race where 10,000-plus runners signed their well-wishes for Bill

Bill's 50th anniversary PTRR trophy

Bill's PTRR Hall of Fame trophy

Coach Bill Thorn's Coaching Career Recap:

52 years as a Georgia high school Head Coach

26 years as a Head Football Coach

45 years as a Head Boys' Track Coach

20 years as a Head Girls' Track Coach

20 years as a Head Boys' and Girls' Cross-Country Coach

4 years as a Head Basketball Coach

2 years as a Head Baseball Coach

THE MAN, THE MYTH, THE LEGEND: A COLLECTION OF STORIES ABOUT BILL THORN

THOUGH WE WANTED TO PUBLISH all collected stories within the chapters, there were so many submitted that we ran out of pages! Please read below for additional memories, laughter, and lessons from Coach Thorn and how his life helped to shape the lives of friends, family, athletes, students, coworkers, and parents.

GEORGIA MILITARY ACADEMY ERA

Bill Curry: Even though I have looked forward to personal visits with Bill through the years and have taken advantage of him by picking his brain each time I was with him, I still had no idea how many championships and honors he had all compiled! I daresay there is no one in our history that has more in sheer volume of accolades, all honorably earned, and all taught with the most stringent codes of discipline, fair play, and team consciousness.

HEADLAND HIGH SCHOOL ERA

Bill Salmond: It was unreal. Coach Thorn did everything. His hard work over time was hard, but over time you could outlast them if you stuck in there. I think that's what he taught everybody. If you stay with it and work hard enough, you may not be the best, but you'll win some trophies. He was right. Our junior and senior years, we were undefeated in track, and dual and trial meets.

Brian Anderson: Coach Thorn was both my football and track coach at Headland High School from 1967-1969. Under his leadership, I had the good fortune of being part of a successful football and track program. To this day, I carry treasured memories of those impressionable high school years and am so thankful to have played for him. Far surpassing the experience of being part of a winning athletic program (which was indeed wonderful) are the invaluable life lessons I learned under Coach Thorn. He passed on to his players the core values that matter throughout life: loyalty, hard work, commitment, and love of life. Words can in no way adequately express my gratitude. I have often tried to analyze what makes a man like Bill Thorn so influential to the young men he coached. I have come to believe that Coach Thorn has a unique "gift from God," and we who played under him were blessed because he was a good steward of that gift.

Charlie Whitehead: He is and always has been so positive about fitness. He was running back when not many people ran. He was a legendary football coach. You knew your school was in great hands with him as head coach.

Ed Salley: I started high school with the full intention/desire to play football and started out on the eighth-grade team (then the B team). I realized that due to my small size at that time, I would likely never play. So I asked Coach Thorn if I could become the equipment manager with my friend, Roger Smith. Coach Thorn welcomed me to this new role, which I cherished from that day until I graduated. He was such a competitor and a winner. I learned a lot of life's lessons from him and the love he had for his teams.

Ellen Denmark: One of the best coaches at Headland. I was never personally coached by him, but I definitely remember how much we all looked up to him. Coach Thorn was a great football coach, always encouraging, and was a great role model and mentor.

Fred Elsberry: Coach was such an inspiration with his work ethic and integrity. My dad knew Coach before he came to Headland, so our families were close, and I even used to babysit his daughters. I got hurt in practice my senior year, so I missed the last part of the season and all of basketball season. Coach kept in touch. He later coached my brother and then coached a competing Landmark track team against my son at Sandy Creek. Coach has been a part of my life for over sixty years.

Jack Slover: He was putting in as much effort as anybody, and you didn't want to let him down. He set the standard. He was right out there with us, and he's done that with all of his students. I was an officer in the military and a lawyer. I was able to deal with some horrible cases because of the toughness he [Coach Thorn] instilled in me. My daddy and Coach Thorn were two of the things that got me through.

Jim "Tex" Harris: Coach Thorn demanded hard work, discipline, and physical conditioning. We gained internal fortitude, integrity, and allegiance to others. Above all, we gained character—something you need to play a sport. I believe character is something that we gravely need in our society today. We need more men like Bill Thorn.

Jim Waller: My first encounter with Coach Bill Thorn was in 1961 when I was a student-athlete in high school. Coach Thorn was a coach at Headland High School with outstanding capabilities in the coaching profession. Even though I was a high school student at this time, I was well aware that we were competing against one of the state's best coaches. Seven years later, I was able to join Coach Thorn at Headland High School on his football staff. It was under Coach Thorn's tutelage that I learned the importance of commitment, dedication, and preparation. Because of Coach Thorn's lessons in coaching and life, I was able to continue on throughout my career, applying similar high standards to all aspects of life and coaching.

Marshall Veal: As our head track and football coach, Bill Thorn always had his players ready to participate, whether we were playing a state football game playoff or running a local track meet. As players, we won many games because we were better prepared than our opponents in mental and physical toughness, excellent conditioning, game strategy, and confidence in our team. Not only was Coach Thorn a successful coach, but even more, he was a great teacher of life lessons. He made sure through the examples of his life that the students and athletes developed abilities that would serve them well for the rest of their lives. As he taught us to respect our teammates and opponents and work harder than our competitors, we developed confidence in our abilities, and we learned if we lost or had a setback, we could get up and try again.

Mickey King: Coach Thorn leads by example. You don't realize that as a young man going through school until you get a little older. You realize how lucky we were to have Coach Thorn as a leader, how he inspired us, and still does. It's almost been sixty years that I was at Hard Labor Creek and still remember a lot of it as if it was yesterday.

Mike Cloy: Bill has always coached for the right reasons. He loves working with young people and helping them to become positive and productive citizens. He loves athletics and the life lessons that it teaches our youth. Most importantly, he realizes that it is all about our youth—not the coaches or the parents, but about the athlete. Coach Thorn is a man of strong religious faith and convictions. He uses this faith to help young people to realize and maximize their true potential for growth and development. He demonstrates the true meaning of the Bible verse Philippians 4:13: "I can do all things through Him that strengthens me." These are some of the values I learned from Bill as a young student-athlete that have remained with me throughout my life: Compete with the will to win and spirit of sportsmanship. Deal with adversity in a positive and productive way; do not give in to adversity, but overcome it. Refuse to lose; be willing to do whatever it takes to compete at the highest level of your being. Life's battles don't always go to the stronger or faster man, but sooner or later, the man who wins is the fellow who thinks he can. Hard work over time defeats talent. You have to be willing to commit to a Total Release Performance—mentally, physically, emotionally, and spiritually. TEAM: Together Everyone Achieves More. Compete with a positive attitude, compete with a great work ethic, be coachable, and—most importantly—be a *we* person, not a *me* person. You must always be willing to persevere, no matter what the circumstances. Most importantly, Bill taught me to do right, not some of the time, but *all* of the time.

Mike Mitchell: Bill Thorn coached at Headland High School from 1959-60 to 1968-69. During that decade of the '60s, Headland had one of the most successful sports programs in the Greater Atlanta Area, and Thorn was one of the keys to that success.

Bill Thorn's Headland teams were not always the most talented, and certainly not the biggest or deepest, but few teams were better prepared technically and mentally, better disciplined, and—most of all—better conditioned. Most of the Briar Boys can still say today that the experience of playing for Bill Thorn and his coaches (Malcolm Moore, Roy Hall, Charley Brown, Jack Short, Larry Whaley, and Jim Waller) was one of their most memorable and impactful in their lives. You may have talent, but do you have the ability, the mental and physical toughness, the character, and the intestinal fortitude to perform (in a coordinated effort) with your full capability in tough, adverse, tense, stressful, and pressured situations? I think most who played for Bill Thorn can answer that. I think the fact that these memories are so strong after fifty-plus years tells how much Bill Thorn is appreciated in my life.

Ronald Logan: Coach had us run four 440s for time, then work on our individual events. As we were on the 220 mark, on the other side of the football field, he would get on the megaphone and yell, "Get the monkey off your back." Then, we would sit in that small section of bleachers, just outside the fence at the goal line, and he would thank us for our dedication. We would have gladly run four more. He was dedicated to our progress. "Quitters never win, and winners never quit," he would tell us.

Theo Caldwell: Coach Thorn's record and outstanding career speak for themselves. He was much more than an outstanding coach. He was a leader and a maker of men. He set a very high standard for all players, both on and off the field. He was fair, extremely knowledgeable, caring, and tough. While at Headland High School, he implemented one of the first and finest strength and conditioning programs in Georgia high school football. He did this in the 1960s before other high schools were using it. Coach Thorn did everything the right way with conviction, compassion, and without compromise. Coach Thorn was responsible for my coaching in Georgia high schools for forty-one years. Every player I coached was influenced by Bill Thorn, and all knew him vicariously through me. He is a man of integrity and a winner.

Tommy Estes: He is a very godly man. I don't remember him ever being late. He was always fair to his players, regardless of how good of an athlete they were. He always ran the teams hard, resulting in Headland players always being in good shape to prepare us to finish strong in the fourth quarter. We ran a lot of wind sprints. Several times, we practiced until dark with a white football so we could see it. He was always prepared for practices and games. He stressed the team to be disciplined and pay attention in practices and meetings, and one time called me out and told the team I was the only one listening (although I'm not sure about that, but I appreciated the compliment). He stressed hard work and expected 100 percent from the team. I will never forget every preseason when the team went to Hard Labor Creek State Park for about a week. We would practice twice a day in the hot sun. The coaches would drive to the "field" (actually just an open, hilly pasture) in an old school bus with the equipment. One morning, some of us decided to hide in a ditch when they drove up. Bad decision—I happened to lie on a yellow jacket nest and got stung about ten times. I thought I might get out of practice but no; I had to practice anyway.

COLONIAL HILLS CHRISTIAN SCHOOL ERA

Jay Russell: Coach Thorn and I go back to 1983 when I was a twenty-four-year-old first-year head football coach, and he had at least thirty years under his belt. Our teams scrimmaged one another that day, and he made a tremendous impression on me. A few weeks later, while having a conversation with my dad, Erk Russell, I brought up Coach Thorn's name, and my dad commented, "He is a good friend and one of the all-time greats." He went on to say that they knew each other well from their days in the 1950s, coaching at their respective Atlanta schools. I have followed Coach Thorn through the years, and his life story is fantastic. I reconnected with him in January of 2015 at the Georgia Track Coaches Clinic. To say that he is the Dean of Track and Field in the state of Georgia would be an understatement. His teams performed at the highest level.

Jeff Doris: I remember football practices being so much harder than the games. You would have thought we were training for a marathon, but we were always well conditioned. When it came to game time, it was almost like a break in that we were in so much better shape than the other team. Even practices in college (at Georgia Tech)—including winter conditioning, spring practice, and summer practice—were not as difficult. And for the record, we did not win as much there as we did in high school. Coach obviously has a special calling for teenagers, but I believe he could have been extremely successful in leading a major college program.

Ray Lamb: I could tell at the first week of football camp with him [Coach Thorn] that he was a guy of high character. Sitting at the dining table talking, I learned he had the same philosophy about football that I did. Strong fundamentals. Lots of coaches do nothing but scheming. But they spend very little time on blocking and tackling. One thing I've noticed about football is that teams that are easy to look at on film and scout and figure out what they are doing sometimes are the toughest teams. You can come up with a defense scheme real easy, but when you get out on the play, they are hard to beat because they are so fundamental. They aren't running many plays, but what they are running, they are running them good. That's the kind of coach I think Bill Thorn was.

Richie Lankford: In the summer of '84, I was transferring to Colonial Hills from the local public school. I met Coach Thorn for the first time, and he said, "What position do you play?" I said quarterback and proceeded to tell him all about my career as an East Point Vol. Coach said, "Hey, those East Point Vols are nothing but a bunch of prima donnas." I knew I was doomed then and there! Coach looked me up and down, pulled out the number thirty-six jersey, and said, "Hey, I'm gonna try you at fullback." A few short weeks later, due to luck and injury, I was starting the first game of the season at quarterback, and Coach said, "Hey, Richie, I got number sixteen if you want it." I stuck with number thirty-six throughout school and threw a last-minute bomb to the legendary Skeeter Stacks for a come-from-behind victory in the season opener. My two seasons playing for Coach Thorn were the best. I have always said he was the only coach I ever had who was as good a coach as my dad was.

Robert Rohm: I entered the world of Coach Thorn a little differently than many of you did. I graduated from college in 1971. I got my first job as the Youth Director at Hillside Baptist Church. I walked in there, and I saw all these young people.

I saw Lynn and Cheryl and Bill and Terry. They were all in my youth group. I was so excited. It was my first job. And I thought I was working as a Youth Director at Hillside Baptist Church. I was as wrong as I could be. I would soon find out I was working for Coach Thorn.

Coach Thorn invited me to meet him at six o'clock in the morning at Greenbrier Mall. And we got to Greenbrier Mall, and we started going inside and running in the mall. He wanted me to learn how to be a runner. I thought, "I'm a Youth Director. I sit in my office and drink coffee and read the Bible. You want me to be at the mall at six o'clock?" Next thing I knew, I was running in the Peachtree Road Race. I ran my very first Peachtree, and it wasn't even really sanctioned back in 1971.

After a while, Coach Thorn began to talk to me, and he helped me to see that being with the young people on Wednesday night and Sunday morning was really not very good. I just didn't see them very often, except Wednesday night at church and Sunday.

Coach Thorn said, "Go over to Headland High School and talk to Mr. Garland Watkins. Mr. Watkins is the principal. You tell him I sent you over there. And you are to be a substitute teacher. If you want to get to know the kids, you have to go to where the kids are. They're at school and not at church." I said, "It makes sense." I went over and talked to Mr. Watkins; he hired me to be a substitute teacher. Next thing I knew, I was at Headland almost every day.

One of the teachers by the name of Mrs. Gun got sick, and I filled in for her. I became a full-time teacher at Headland High School. Well, Coach Thorn said, "Let's start a Bible study in my home." So we started a Bible study. I was the math teacher at Headland High School. I would tell them, "If you come to my Bible study on Thursday night, I'm going to have a special math review for the test after Bible study." Word got out that I basically went over the whole test. We had a couple hundred kids come into their [the Thorns'] house on Thursday night for Bible study. One night, we had a pizza party. We had 200 pizzas. I'm sharing the Gospel and giving them pizza afterward. We had pizza in the Bible study, the house, the bushes. Coach Thorn was buying pizza for years after that.

FAYETTE CHRISTIAN SCHOOL ERA

Jason Settle: We never went into a game thinking, "Well, we don't have enough guys", "We don't have the best facilities" or "We play in this particular conference." He may have felt that way, but in his mind, we always entered thinking, "We're about to win this game." We may not have won it, but let me tell you, we put in so much work, it was a joy for us to get together and say, "Hey, let's go lift. Hey, let's go run. Hey, let's get into agility drills." He was doing plyometrics before plyometric boxes were a thing. We're jumping on old metal bleacher seats, and he's telling us, "I don't want to hear your feet hit the bleacher. Make sure to bend those knees to land soft like a cat." He was making us do lateral jumps to build side strength in our knees back in '86.

Roby Ross: It's never too late for God to do great things throughout your life. I met him when he was in his mid-50s. After that time, he started Landmark, won countless state championships, and impacted the lives of hundreds of kids over my twenty-four years of coaching with him.

When Coach Thorn says something to you, his words have power. I think the reason why this is, is this—he never praised mediocrity. He'd never give out meaningless accolades. He's also not a coach who would just yell for the sake of yelling. When he quietly told you that you weren't giving your best effort, it was devastating. Because when he said it, we knew it was true.

LANDMARK CHRISTIAN SCHOOL ERA

Adam Hanes: I played football and ran track with Coach Thorn. We were lined up to play Bremen my junior year for homecoming with a huge crowd, great night, perfect weather, and everything you could dream up for a football game. We were warming up, and somebody came over and talked to Coach Thorn. And I remember thinking, "What are they talking about?" Coach Thorn came over, and he said, "Hey, take off your cleats; go get your running shoes. Refs aren't showing tonight. The game is canceled. Line up, boys; we're running the mile." I'm thinking, "What? This is homecoming. No, that's not what we're supposed to do." No lies, as they're announcing the homecoming queen, we're on the track running our mile. This is the one time I thought I might quit. We had a full practice after that mile; we ran through the whole thing, missed the dance, and missed everything that night. Looking back on it now, I realize there are going to be things that don't go your way. There are going to be things that come up. There are always obstacles. One thing I can say about Coach Thorn is that he is a very determined man. Some people might say stubborn.

I have six kids. One of the things I've told them now every day was to be good at anything, you have to work hard. Stuff doesn't go your way. I hate when they tell me, "That's not fair." Life's not fair. When you want to do something, you have to be determined. You have to stick to it, and you have to go with it.

Coach Thorn, thank you. What you've taught me will go on for generations now because those are the same things I'm teaching my kids, and several others are doing the same thing. It's going to carry on through eternity.

Archie Burgess: Favorite Thornism: "When you become complacent is when others have beaten you."

Ben Stout: I was so blessed to have known Coach since I was maybe four or five years old. Basically, my whole childhood, I wanted to play ball and run track for Coach. Growing up in Dr. Dial's church every Sunday, I'd want to know if Coach won or lost. He coached a lot of the men in the church—Dan Lee and Eric Dial among them. Once I finally was able to get coached, it was intense. After a rough week or months, I called Eric Dial and asked him some questions. The biggest one being, "Why does Coach yell at me so much?" The response was that if Coach stops getting on you and "yelling," he's given up on you. I remember telling Eric, "Well, he certainly has a lot of belief in me."

Brad Eisenburg: After every cross-country meet, we would always go to Ryan's or Golden Corral, and we would always tell the server that it was Coach's birthday. They would come out singing and cheering, and every time he laughed (even if it had just happened the week before). Coach Thorn was a tough coach, but no one was more gracious than him. It's Coach Thorn whom I have modeled my leadership skills after. There were numerous times when I tried to quit and leave the team; every time I realized I made a mistake, and he welcomed me back with open arms because he truly cared about his athletes.

Camden Cusumano: Because Coach Thorn was very honest and old-school, he was never one to flatter or give compliments freely. I remember one day, after a very hard workout, he told me, "Boy, you aren't afraid of hard work, are you?" Thinking I was receiving a compliment for completing the workout, I said, "No, sir, I'm not." Coach Thorn replied with a grin: "That's right—you'll lay down right beside it."

Eddie Waggoner: Bill has spread the Gospel to hundreds, if not thousands, of young people. And not only to the young people but to their parents. All the time, he's talking to everybody about Jesus Christ. When we get older, we're not measured by what position we have. We're not measured by how much money we have accumulated. We're not measured by how many wins or losses we've got. And we're not measured by how many trophies or awards we got. We're measured by one thing and one thing only, Jesus Christ, and if you've accepted him as your Lord and Savior.

Vince Cobb: What is a champion? Someone who is unwilling to change the way that they win. Great preachers, teachers, and coaches have a lot in common. They measure their time frame because you only have so much time to minister Jesus and convince them (students/athletes) to be excellent. Coach Thorn would probably say, "If you don't know Jesus, don't waste any more of your time doubting because he's ready for you right now." It was always about how we loved Jesus and how we coached and ministered to young people. Coach is and was a hardliner. He stayed true to his program. He had one program that had a narrow path, saying, "It's hard, but it's right." Coach ministered to kids daily, encouraging them in the faith. His strict training regimen helped to win so many state championships and create several state champions. What I like most about Coach Thorn is that his at-all-costs, never-give-up, push-all-the-way-through mentality grew young men and women into very strong young adults. You didn't have to be a state champion or be on a state championship team to learn about his winning attitude. We got along really well because he and I were in alignment as coaches and men who love God.

Cathy Thames: There are simply no words to describe the impact this man has made on me and my family. My kids, Chad and Ryan, continue to draw on the foundation Coach Thorn instilled in each of them. Coach Thorn stood strong when many would have folded. He instilled dedication and strength and expected that of his athletes. He had our backs on and off the field. He is truly the greatest man of integrity I know.

Chris Fegans: Because of our daughters' passion and motivation to excel in distance running, we wanted to make sure they would have the absolute best coaching to squeeze all the talent out of them at the high school level. Between friends who recommended Landmark and my research, Coach Thorn's program looked like a great fit. We walked into a dream situation on the first day.

Nicole was our oldest, who started Landmark in 2013. During Nicole's freshman year of cross-country, she trained alongside sophomore teammate Kathryn Foreman and had the chance to see how Coach Thorn's program really worked, and the effort required, as Kathryn won the 2013 Georgia Gatorade Runner of the Year as the number one female runner in the state. With this, Coach Thorn had our girls go on a five-year state championship run. In 2016, Erin—our youngest—joined the Landmark cross-country team, which turned out to be Georgia's fastest high school women's cross-country team in history. That year, Coach Thorn coached Nicole up to also become the 2016 Georgia Gatorade Runner of the Year. No high school in Georgia has had two female Gatorade Runners of the Year like Landmark. Nicole was also ranked number seven in the nation thanks to our great program. In 2016, our Landmark girls' cross-country team won the Georgia Meet of Champions, making them number one in Georgia "all classifications." Our little 1A school was number one in a team sport of five! Not only that, but we still hold the fastest average team time for a high school girls' 5K all-time (18:43!). I'd say Coach Thorn got all the talent out of our girls, as they both have moved on with the knowledge and work ethic he instilled to be successful at the next level.

Christian McGuire Wade: I ran for Coach Thorn for four seasons of track and begrudgingly for three seasons of cross-country. Growing up, I was a soccer player. When I came to Landmark, all of my friends were runners, so I decided as a freshman to give track a shot. I ended up running as an alternate on the 4x4 team that year and earned my first state championship ring. From there, I was somehow convinced to run cross-country with a promise that it would make me a better sprinter—it did. Throughout the years that I ran for Coach Thorn—or Pop Pop as my teammates and I called him because we were on the team with and friends with his granddaughter, Kenzie—I improved as a runner and went on to win four individual state championships in the 100-meter and 300-meter hurdles my junior and senior years. I was on three state championship cross-country teams and two state-championship track teams. If you just look at the results, you would probably think that I was an easy kid to coach and that I did what I was told when I was told. I was quite a handful for Coach Thorn and Coach Ross through the years. I even got kicked out of a practice on my birthday one year. I don't remember what I did, but I am sure I deserved it.

By the time I got to my junior year, I was in great shape and was set to win both hurdles and compete on both relay teams. That year, the winner of the 4x4 would become state champions. For Landmark to win, we had to win the 4x4. For context, the 4x4 was right after the 300m hurdles and I would have to run up the stadium to the bus to ice my legs in between the two events. There was very little time to do this, but I always made it back just before my team took the track. That year, I was the final leg of that relay team, and I watched as my team got further and further behind. I got handed the baton in second place, trailing by about twenty meters or so. I still have no idea how, but I caught her! I was running the final 100, and she was getting closer and closer. As we approached the finish line, it was neck-and-neck. I passed out as I crossed the finish line, and remember one of the officials saying, "That's the girl who just won the hurdles; get her off the track."

I vaguely remember getting half-carried off of the track and taken to the medical tent, where my teammates came to wait with me to hear the results. It turned out that we lost by 0.03 of a second. I was crushed. I felt like I had let the team down, and like a "grown-up" seventeen-year-old, I went straight to my mom and cried my eyes out in her lap. I was so upset. I had lost for the whole team. What would Coach Thorn say? Now, you might wonder why I would choose a story of loss to share here, and the reason is simple. To Coach Thorn and Coach Ross that day, we won. They saw that all of the lectures and all of the hard days when I gave them so much trouble had been worth it. I literally left it *all* on the track that day for my teammates. I gave it my very best, and that was all that they ever asked of me. So as I walked, head hung low, expecting disappointment, you can imagine my surprise when I was embraced and told, "I have never been more proud of you."

It changed everything. It changed me. I learned so much about life that day. I learned so much about Jesus and his love for his people by watching Coach Thorn and Coach Ross celebrate my teammates and me, not necessarily as runners, but as young women preparing to enter the real world. I finally grasped that all of the lessons that they were trying to teach us went so far beyond the 400 meters of rubber. They were teaching us to be strong and resilient, to face life head-on, and to "leave it all on the track," so to say. They were teaching us about life this whole time.

Even though I was a mess and got myself into loads of trouble, Coach Thorn told me years later that I was good trouble, which I take as a compliment. Those years were formative for the person that I have become. Coach Thorn could have written me off as a troublemaker or given up on me, but he never did. He constantly stayed on my case because he knew who I could be. He knew that I was just a kid figuring out my place in the world and that he could teach me lessons on the track that would translate to every area of my life. To this day, I have "Thornisms" running through my mind when times get tough. "When it's too hard for others, it's just right for us." "Hard work, given time, defeats talent." Over the past few years, a small group of us have done almost monthly "Coach Thorn dinners," as we call them. We gather together and listen to the wisdom; we laugh now at the trouble I caused, and occasionally Coach Thorn will show us the workouts that he is doing these days—once a coach, always a coach. As for me, I am so glad that Pop Pop gets to see the person I have grown into because so many of the good parts of who I am, I owe to him.

Clark Rivers: I had the privilege of running for Coach Thorn for five years and coaching against him for a decade. In my opinion, the mark of a great coach is the ability to get the most out of their athletes, regardless of gender or ability. Coach Thorn had an uncanny ability to take average athletes, and over time, develop them to a level where they were competing (and often winning) at the state championship level. When fortune shined on him and gifted athletes came through his program, state records were broken, and the teams were the best in the state, regardless of classification. A remarkable feat, considering Landmark's very small size. From the standpoint of measurable achievements, state championships, elite performances, etc., Coach Thorn's record is far and away the best in the history of the state of Georgia.

Regarding what is not measurable, Coach Thorn was a master. Everyone on the team was treated equally, whether they were the fastest runner in the state or a freshman running for the first time. His focus was on the journey and the approach needed each day to be great at the state championship. Young people need direction and consistency. Coach Thorn provided both in spades and expected the same out of his athletes. Be at practice every day, no excuses. Run the workout the way it was designed to the best of your ability. There were no off days. I ran for three years without a day off, and I had many teammates who had similar consistent day streaks. Knowing that I was working toward a common goal with my coaches and teammates kept me going every day. Plus, if I didn't, Coach Thorn was sure to address it with me in a firm but loving manner.

The feeling at the end of the season, running the 4x400m relay at the state meet in Jefferson with my friends and teammates, knowing we were about to win another championship, is indescribable. Not because we finished first, but because I was just an average kid in seemingly every way, including running. Guys like me don't win state championships. Coach

Thorn provided that gift to me. He made me realize that if I give my best effort, and *truly* give my best effort, over time, great things will happen. This man changed the trajectory of my life for the better, and I will forever be grateful.

Heather Hayes: Coach Thorn was always a pusher, even when—and especially when—he knew you weren't confident in yourself. He could see your potential before you could. I remember when he asked me to run the 800m and the mile (with a slight grin, I might add!). I did not want to run either, and he knew I didn't want to run them. However, he asked if I could try and see how it went. I ended up making it to state in the 800m and getting very close to breaking Landmark's record. I never knew that was possible. He always had a smile on his face, even if you didn't. He was proud of everything we did as individuals and as a team.

His Thornisms were one of a kind, and I still use them to this day! He made you want to work harder, push your limits, and become an incredible athlete. Watching him exercise on his mini trampoline when we went to State was so inspiring; he practiced what he preached! As serious as he was when it was training time, he also knew when to have fun. Going to Gulf Shores for spring break, catching the bread rolls at Lambert's restaurant, watching him dance with Mrs. Patty, and listening to his funny stories and jokes will be memories I will never forget.

I wouldn't be where I am today without his guidance and support. Between his perseverance and dedication as a coach/teacher, husband to Mrs. Patty, and a man of God, he will forever be a man that will go down in history.

Judy Titus: One year at the sports banquet, Mike (my husband) got up to introduce Coach. He had a large stack of old computer paper that was attached that had to be torn apart after each page. He said a line, then flung the paper over the podium. We all got a laugh. Coach Thorn was well known for his long-winded speeches.

Kaity Bulger: Once, in high school, I skipped a weekend workout. I came to practice on Monday and told Coach. He wasn't mad, but he looked at me and said, "You know you're going to have to do two workouts today, right?" I was going to have to run six miles' worth of intervals, then do another interval path right after. It was a really long, hard day. It sounds miserable, but Coach Thorn knew what he was doing; he did it for me. This was the perfect lesson when you make mistakes in life: There are consequences.

Katey Lewis: I never gave in, but Coach asked me every time in the hall to consider field events with his track team. My response was, "I'll do it, but I hate running . . . so if you're going to make me run, count me out." His response was always, "Anyone can run; your response to it is mental." And while I never ran track, and I never did track events, that phrase stuck with me throughout my volleyball coaching career.

Kelsie McDuffie: I have so many favorite memories of running for Coach Thorn. One of my favorites would occur every year at the beginning of track season. So many eager kids would come out for track conditioning, having heard of the wonder that was Coach Thorn. Each day that passed, there would be fewer and fewer kids showing up for practice. You'd hear them in class the next day, complaining about how sore they were and how they just couldn't do it. About two weeks in, you'd look around and the folks remaining were the ones who you knew could hang and would be your team members for the rest of the season. It always made me giggle inside with how many people couldn't handle it. It would be about that time when Coach would say, "When it's too tough for others, it's just right for us." It made you feel proud inside that you accomplished something a lot of others couldn't. You and your teammates had an unspoken bond and mutual respect that you were doing something really hard, day in and day out. At the end of the day, it all comes down to that mental toughness he preached. Since then, there've been many times in life where I've thought to myself, "If I could run for Coach Thorn, I can get through this too." Running for Coach Thorn felt like a rite of passage.

Lauren Toomer Moton: Coach Thorn is not one of the best track coaches I've ever had . . . he is *the* best coach I've ever had. I started running track when I came to Landmark in sixth grade until twelfth grade. My younger brother, Nicolas, also ran track at Landmark. After high school, I continued my collegiate track career at Georgia Southern University. Coach Thorn's philosophy of no excuses, hard work, dedication, and tough love spans over the many, many, many years of his coaching tenure. Coach Thorn was always instilling words of godly wisdom to all his runners and making us tough our way through the grueling workouts. Although some of the workouts made us question why we wanted to run track in the first place, the positive results spoke for themselves. There was a true buy-in from each runner to believe in what we were doing and actually have fun doing it. We learned that when it was too hard for others, it's just right for us. We were always ready for anything.

A funny story I have is from a day in practice. We were doing our usual running, and someone came up to Coach Thorn and said, "Coach, I threw up." And he quickly responded, "All right, I guess you ought to feel better now. Get goin'." There was literally no excuse you could get past Coach Thorn. He always had us laughing with his witty remarks. The banquet speeches . . . Let's just say, if you know, you know. Coach Thorn's handwritten notes and stats on every single person amazed me. The attention to detail was immaculate. He read everything he wrote, no matter how long it took. Since my last race as a Landmark athlete, Coach Thorn and Mrs. Patty have been to both my brothers' and my graduation parties and attended my wedding in June 2022. Although I don't get to see them often, after all the years that have passed since my Landmark days, they still feel like family. I will forever be grateful for and will love the Thorns.

Marlon Bryan: The whole season had been building to this moment, to this race. I knew before the race began, I would have to do something drastic to win this race. I was mentally ready to win at any cost. Moments before the race, I was getting set up to run, and I kept hearing Coach's voice in my head: "Leave it all out on the track, or you'll always regret it." I knew I'd be running for more than just a medal that day. As I was running, I thought about my grandfather; my brother, Ian; my mom; Coach Thorn; and Coach Ross—everyone who helped me get to that race. As we came down the final stretch, I knew I'd be diving for the finish. I started adjusting my stride so that I could dive off of my dominant leg. I thought that at worst, I'd place second, but if I dove, I could win. After the race, they had to postpone the awards ceremony so they could triple-check the finish. I had won by .03 of a second.

I had that drive to win because of Coach Thorn. When I first came to Landmark, Coach Thorn was one of the first people I met. He'd never seen me run before, but as soon as we met, he said, "You're going to be my next state championship hurdler." His belief in me was shocking—he'd never seen me run but already knew I was going to be great. I think that's one of his greatest gifts—to see the truth and greatness in people even if they can't see it for themselves. He pulls it out of them through hard work and dedication, exactly like he would do. He didn't ask any more of us than he was willing to do himself. No matter the problem, nobody worked as hard as he did, and he did it all with patience and compassion.

The rarity of this coach is he cut time, and he got serious about becoming better. Difference makers are special. They start somewhere wanting to know how things work. They find the things that work. And a difference maker is always a teacher first. They teach first and coach second. You impart knowledge that nobody else is getting from anybody. Coach Thorn did that.

Matthew Thornton: After my father passed, he came over to me at graduation and said to never give up and to never quit the long race in life that I have ahead. I plan on running a full Ironman in honor of him and my late father. I'm thankful to be back on track because of folks like Bill who poured into my life.

Melanie Farmer: Other than my own father, Coach Thorn was the most influential man in my youngest son's life. As a single mother of two sons in 2003, and as a resident of Clayton County, where SACS had placed the school system on probation for accreditation, I was desperately in search of a school where my youngest son could not only reach his potential but flourish. Brett had never been a great student but had always been an excellent runner. I learned of Coach Thorn through some coworkers and ultimately decided that, although I couldn't afford it, Landmark Christian was the best place for Brett. From the very first moment I met Coach Thorn, I knew I had made the right decision. I had never met a man who cared more for these athletes than Coach Thorn, nor have I met one since.

One of the things that impressed me the most was his desire for each athlete to know the Lord first and succeed in life second. He used coaching as a means to this end. He prepared a personal training schedule for each student every single day based on their performance the day before. His expectations of each runner were very high, and he held them to those expectations. One of the most impressive things to me was his commitment to excellence in his own life.

He didn't just stand on the sidelines and "tell" the students what they should be doing as far as training and diet; he modeled it. He was and is a very fit man. No student could ever say of him that he was a "Do as I say, not as I do" kind of coach. His commitment to my son and his daily investment in his life for three years ultimately led Brett to bring his mile time down to 4:23 and got him a scholarship to Troy University to run track and cross country. Brett also achieved two high school state championship titles in cross-country and six region titles in cross-country and track combined under Coach Thorn's leadership. Most importantly, Coach Thorn helped Brett believe in himself.

Mike Titus: You could always tell the new kids to the track or cross-country program. When there was bad weather, they would say, "They're going to cancel practice today." Of course, the veteran kids would laugh. It didn't matter what the weather was like out there; they were going to practice. Back in those days, we didn't care about lightning. If it didn't hit you, you just kept on going.

Natalie Toomer: Landmark's track team was participating in a meet at Marist High School. The weather was bad, with lots of rain and thunder. It was initially delayed, then ultimately canceled. Coach had his team wait out the storm, and when it had subsided, the team ran 4x400 relays . . . the whole team. All the other teams had gone home, even the host school's team and staff! Our family still laughs about that meet now.

On another note, Coach Thorn has been a great man of faith who stands by his word no matter what. He has a special heart and has poured immensely into our family. He is one that you have to get to know . . . we know, adore, and love him. He's been a part of our family for about seventeen years by way of Landmark Christian School. Much of our time together was through the track team and included the famous Gulf Shores trips. We have so many fond memories from those trips and enjoyed listening to his many stories about previous trips and his life stories. Not many people know it, but Coach is hilarious. As family members do, he has come to all of our kids' celebrations—from high school and college graduations, to a wedding last year. There are not enough pages to cover what he means to so many of us. We love him and are so blessed to have him in our lives.

Olivia Bouchard: All of the Thornisms really suit him. A few key things stick out to me: all the time he devoted to his speeches and time during practice. He created an awesome environment for kids to make friends. My best memories weren't necessarily with him, but because of the things he did. Coach brought us all to Gulf Shores, and I had so much fun with my teammates. He scheduled races close to the river, and we'd all go swimming afterward. He let us run in the woods, where we all had so much fun running and talking to each other. My teammates were my best friends.

A memory I'll never forget, and he never let me live down, was during my time at Landmark, when they needed an extra runner to make a middle school cross-country team. I had no training whatsoever, but I went out there. I didn't realize you're not supposed to eat a lot before races, but I had a ton of watermelon before. Needless to say, I puked over all the competitors as we raced to the finish line. After that, Coach told us before every meet, how we needed to have toast with almond butter and blueberries. That's it. He *always* told us not to overeat and made an example out of it for years. It was hilarious.

Rachel Morley: There are so many stories to share that Coach Thorn taught his athletes. The number one thing I remember and share with my athletes for track and field and volleyball is, "Winners find a way." No matter what the circumstances, Coach Thorn taught me to push through. His tough love and discipline impacted me then, and I still remember and apply his lessons today.

Randy Gravitt: As a parent of four of Coach Thorn's athletes, I always appreciated the fact that he pushed them to be their very best. While they won championships and received accolades, it was his emphasis on godly character that I admired most.

Scott Neal: As followers of Jesus, it is important to hold each other accountable. I think that also means sharing the positives when it is evident that the Holy Spirit works through people. I've often shared with Coach Thorn and Coach Ross my admiration and respect for the culture they have created in the Landmark track program. I've also often shared with others, including my teams, every year, the "knack" the kids at Landmark have to perform for each other. It is common every year at the state meet to see a distinct surge in performance—I believe more so than other schools—and it seems that it is driven by a common bond to do one's best because it is needed and counted on beyond a trophy. The trophy, it seems, is just an external rallying point for what God can do through each of them.

Stockton McGuire: When I was in the eighth grade, a couple of my buddies and I were hurdling at practice. Coach Thorn was helping us with our block starts and going over the first hurdle. One particular rep, my buddy Taylor Snyder, went over the first hurdle and unfortunately got both of his legs caught up in the top of the hurdle and—at full speed—went face-first into the track. It was a pretty brutal fall, but of course, we were trying not to laugh. After a few seconds went by, Coach Thorn just looked at Taylor and said, "There's a hurdle there, boy," in his calm Coach Thorn voice. We lost it with uncontrollable laughter. We still quote that to this day, and probably will forever. Coach Thorn was a tough man with a dry sense of humor, and he loved all of us much better than we deserved because he knew he was loved by Christ much better than he deserved. His life was a living testimony of love and bearing the cross daily. I am forever grateful for his impact on my life.

Wendy Regan: Coach Thorn is a godly man of good character. He consistently models the Christlike behavior, good work ethic, positive attitude, and commitment to fitness that he expects of his athletes. I went to practices several days a week and to every meet for years. I never heard of or saw him "lose it" with any athlete or parent. He models the compassionate professionalism that many others lack. His standards are high, but fair and consistent.

PEACHTREE ROAD RACE AND OTHER PERSONAL AND PROFESSIONAL CONNECTIONS

Andy Carr: I have known Coach Thorn for nearly thirty years, and besides respect, astonishment, and absolute honor of him, he is just plain down to earth. My best memory is when he called me to ask about coming to race his top girls on the Milton HS XC course, one of the toughest and slowest in the state. He wanted to know every detail, turn, surface, etcetera, and once he was satisfied, he basically said: "Hot, hill, hard, or easy, it's the same for everyone. Time doesn't matter in cross-country; it's who you can beat on any given day." That is what made his runners the best competitors. We [Milton] didn't get to race Landmark many times while Coach Thorn was there, but when we did, we knew they were bringing their best and were going to "throw down" on everyone they raced that day. A Coach Thorn athlete is just not a good runner; they are a good person. They will give it their all and are most respectful to all their competitors, just like Coach Thorn was to all of us opposing coaches and teams.

Beth Dial: The question is often asked, "Where would Coach Thorn be without Patty?" The primary answer is that Patty has an insatiable hunger for God's word, in which we learn to lay down our lives as Christ did for us. Back in the '70s, she rarely missed a Bible study taught by Howard Dial or Mrs. Horton. She and Bill joined Berachah Bible Church, pastored by Dr. Dial, and still regularly take their places on the front row.

An interesting example of Patty's love of scripture was many years ago. As she was driving and listening to Dr. J. Vernon McGee teaching his "Through the Bible" series, so that she wouldn't miss a word, her Bible was open beside her to the book of Ephesians. She swerved, hit a transformer telephone pole, and knocked out her two front teeth. She wanted to go to church that Sunday, but Bill would have none of that. Later, Dr. McGee was preaching in the area. After the message, Patty approached him to tell him what had happened. With his quick wit and inimitable Texas drawl, he replied, "Well, that'll teach you never to look down on Ephesians."

Bob Dalton: Like most people, I first heard of Bill Thorn through his reputation as the only person to race in every Peachtree Road Race, held annually on the Fourth of July. I learned further of his reputation as a superb coach and mentor through his many winning teams in both cross-country and track at Landmark. I have known Coach Thorn for approximately twenty years. As an assistant coach at one of the other high schools in the same county, we often saw each other at various track and cross-country meets and became friends over the years.

During that time, I have looked to him as a role model. I can tell you that the other coaches revered him for his wisdom and experience. During my own career in the US Army, I coached the West Point Marathon Team from 1990-1992, the Ft. McPherson Army Ten Miler Team from 1996-2012, and served as a coach for the Atlanta Track Club from 2011-2014. So, I can understand and appreciate the time and effort Bill has put into coaching excellence. But more than that, he has poured his life into young men and women using track and cross-country as a metaphor for life. You have successes and failures along the way, but no matter what, you get back up and keep going.

Emory B. Fears: During the years that Bill Thorn has coached, he has inspired his runners to do their best, which has resulted in many state championships in boys' and girls' cross-country and track. Bill has also used his knowledge of running to help other coaches become more knowledgeable about the sport. I had the opportunity to coach against Bill for ten years and during that time, his teams were well coached and demonstrated good sportsmanship. Bill is well respected by other coaches—as well as runners—who have had the opportunity to learn from him as he coached them to victory.

Ken Sugiura: I've gotten to know Coach Thorn as a writer who covers the Peachtree Road Race. It's amazing to me . . . Most of Atlanta knows Coach Thorn for his association with the world's largest 10K. He's the guy who was running all of them. There's only one person in the world who has done that. And you know, people celebrate him for that (rightfully so). And yet, everyone here at the Coach Thorn Gala is like, "That doesn't matter." He's had so much of an impact on all of you and hundreds and thousands more not in this room. One thing that was said that resonated with me was "You're the most disciplined man I've met." I can certainly see how that happens. To have done any one of those things would, as I said, be something worth celebrating. To have that full life and to have that sort of influence on so many people and so many hearts and souls, you can't put any sort of measure on that.

AFTERWORD

BY CHUCK CUSUMANO

THE BILL THORN PROJECT: MORE THAN JUST A BOOK

THE "WHY": A MISSION BEYOND A MEMOIR

"PROJECT" ISN'T A CASUAL LABEL HERE. Diving into Bill Thorn's world is like stepping into a whirlwind—it's never just a simple story. What started as a "Let's write a book" idea quickly morphed into a full-blown expedition, a quest to capture the essence of a man whose influence ripples far beyond any page.

My 2016 attempt? Eight hours of interviews later, and I was floored. This wasn't just a biography; it was an undertaking that demanded a team, a mission. I thought I knew Coach Thorn, but his life was a series of jaw-dropping intersections, a real-life Forrest Gump story.

Picture this: seventy-five years young, and Coach Thorn is still on the field, molding athletes. Forget retirement; he's racking up state championships and inspiring kids like my daughter Kaley. My initial image of a towering, booming coach? Shattered. He was a five-foot-two force of nature, radiating seriousness and genuine care. Think Mickey from *Rocky* but with a twinkle in his eye and a stack of practice notes thicker than a phone book.

Seventeen years. That's how long my family was immersed in the Bill Thorn experience. My kids ran for him, my wife taught at his school, and I got a front-row seat to his relentless drive. He built a school, a legacy, on faith, grit, and a knack for turning "impossible" into "done."

"Why do you keep telling me all these things?" I asked him once. "Because when I mention it to you, it gets done," he replied, with that signature glint. That's when I knew this story had to be told, before it vanished like footprints in the sand.

THE "HOW": WEAVING A TAPESTRY OF VOICES

This isn't just a biography; it's a chorus of voices, a collection of moments that paint a vivid portrait of Coach Thorn's impact. We chased down athletes, parents, rivals—anyone who had a "Bill Thorn story." It's a testament to the ripple effect of a life lived with purpose. And guess what? The story's still unfolding.

We dove headfirst into Coach Thorn's archives—a chaotic but magnificent treasure trove of records, photos, and enough paper to fill a small library. His meticulous notes were a gold mine, but turning them into a cohesive narrative? That required a team, a band of storytellers and data wranglers.

THE "WHO": A SCRAPPY SQUAD OF STORYTELLERS, DATA WRANGLERS, AND DREAM WEAVERS

Putting together this project felt like assembling a championship team, Coach Thorn style: driven, resourceful, and ready to tackle any challenge.

Jillian Broaddus (The Architect of Narrative): Jillian wasn't just a writer; she was a time traveler, weaving together hours of interviews and mountains of notes into a cohesive narrative. She meticulously researched historical context, breathing life into the past and ensuring every detail was accurate. And she built www.CoachBillThorn.com, a digital hub for memories and stories, proving her versatility and dedication. She truly built the backbone of this book.

Brandi Belveal (The Polish and Push): Like a seasoned sprinter in the final lap, Brandi took the almost-finished manuscript and injected it with clarity and polish. She was the essential translator, ensuring Coach Thorn's voice and the stories resonated with authenticity. She didn't just edit; she elevated the entire project.

Deb Kay (The Digital Detective): Deb was our internet sleuth, uncovering hidden gems and building timelines that illuminated Coach Thorn's journey. She transformed scattered online information into valuable insights, managed our social media outreach, and spearheaded the monumental task of digitizing Coach Thorn's vast collection. She bridged the gap between the analog and digital worlds.

Tamara Bowen (The Maestro of Organization): In a world of overflowing papers and countless interviews, Tamara was our compass. She orchestrated meetings, coordinated Zoom calls, and tamed the chaos of Coach Thorn's archives. More than just a scheduler, she was the glue that held us together, a vital liaison and a master of keeping everyone on track.

Hanna Marcus (The Heart and Soul): Hanna wasn't just refining sentences; she was capturing the essence of Coach Thorn's spirit. She conducted in-depth interviews, ensuring the stories were told with sensitivity and depth. She wove Coach Thorn's faith into the narrative, making sure his convictions resonated with every reader. Her dedication to honoring Coach's voice was paramount.

Caleb Stanley (The Visual Bard): Caleb transformed Coach Thorn's world into a visual story, capturing the essence of his legacy through his lens. He documented the artifacts, the papers, and the memories and created compelling video content for our social media outreach. His ability to capture the right shot, every time, was nothing short of miraculous (with vital assistance from Tyler Kangas and Jordan Griffe, who added invaluable video production expertise for the website and gala).

Chuck Cusumano (The Spark Plug): I was the instigator, the one who dared to ask, "What if we told this story?" I assembled this incredible team, conducted interviews, and navigated the challenges of bringing this vision to life. My role was to ensure the story was not only told, but told with the respect, accuracy, and passion it deserved.

This team, a diverse collection of talents and personalities, mirrored the very essence of a Bill Thorn team: driven, resourceful, and forever changed by the experience. We didn't just write a book; we became a part of the Bill Thorn legacy.

ACKNOWLEDGMENTS

BILL THORN and the Bill Thorn Book Project want to thank the following people and organizations who made this book possible. Without your generous contributions, support, and attendance, this project would not have been possible.

Patty Thorn
Lynn Victor
Cheryl Thrasher
Steve Thrasher
Bill Thorn Jr.
Terry Thorn
Natalie Williams
Kenzie Bayman
Max Bayman
Kerri Sanders
Sarah Thorn
Dr. John Till
Andrew Cathy
Mandy Cathy
Lauren McGuire
Perry McGuire
Christian McGuire Wade
Tanner Wade
Lauren McGuire Grimsley
Justin Grimsley
Reed McGuire
Rachel McGuire
Stockton McGuire
Addie McGuire
Eric Quint
Lorri Swords
Marshall Veal
Rivertown Group
Alison Guerard
Turner Guerard
Matt Thornton
Brett Lewis
David Wilkins
Stephen Wilkins
Monica Wilkins
Brenda Wilkins
Jonathan Wilkins
Leanne Wilkins
Ian Wilkins
Dawn Fegans
Nicole Fegans
Erin Fegans
Fred Fegans
Jessie Heath
Brandon Heath
Howard Dial
Beth Dial
Andee Ellerbee

David Harkins
Jill Harkins
Jim “Tex” Harris
Brenda Harris
Sherry Kangas
Tim Kangas
Tyler Kangas
Mickey King
Tommy McDaniel
Sharon McDaniel
Cheryl Parker
Steve Parker
Keely Schmidlkofer
Madison Schmidlkofer
Natalie Toomer
La’Mont Toomer
Wanda Waggoner
Eddie Waggoner
Daniel Wesche
Emily Wesche
Jimmy Jordan
Hannah Gravitt May
Trevor May
Janet Monk
Tim Monk
Lauren Moton
Bo Causey
Harold Mims
Brian Anderson
Coach Jim Waller
Greg Ward
Stephen Wilkins
Mike Cloy
Kyle Gable
Marty Riggs
Mike Bell
William Bolton
Gary Butler
Richard Greer
Jim King
Steven Ray
Stephen Weeks
Eddie Anderson
Tom Jenkins
Jeff Payne
Tamara Bowen
Marshall Sellers
Andy Anderson
Drew Anderson
Robin Anderson
Jon Bridges
Amy Bridges
Jillian Broaddus
Jane Broaddus
Ra Broaddus
Randal Bryan
Sara Bryan
Missy Bryan
Micah Carver
Anna Lisa Chavez
Wes Bowen
Vince Cobb
Lori Cobb
Donald Crabtree
Gwen Crabtree
Chuck Cusumano
Katie Cusumano
Kierstin Cusumano
Camden Cusumano
Natalie Keohane
Melanie Farmer
Betty Gebhardt

Fred Gilkeson
Shelia Gilkeson
Kaley Glenn
Jordan Griffie
Heather Hayes
Linda Hayes
Deb Kay
Pat King
Mario Latasa
Dana Latasa
Sydney Miller
Scott Patman
Kathy Patman
Jackie Reed
Steve Reed
Connor Reynolds
Durand Rice
Robert Rohm
Ron Ross
Glenda Ross
Marie Snyder
Jeffrey Snyder
Caleb Stanley
Masey McLain
Ken Sugiura
Robyn Sugiura
Cathy Thames
Barry Williams
Carol Williams
Jeremy Williams
Dennis Williams
Earl Winfrey
Michael Winfrey
Wil Winfrey
Michaela Winfrey
Gary Wood
Kathy Wood
Hanna Woods
Riley Woods

Coach Thorn would like to extend a special thank-you to Lauren R. McGuire for her generous financial contributions, which made this book possible.

A Gala Event Celebrating
Coach Bill Thorn

A Gala Event Celebrating
Coach Bill Thorn

A Gala Event Celebrating
Coach Bill Thorn

A Gala Event Celebrating
Coach Bill Thorn

A Gala Event Celebrating
Coach Bill Thorn

Snapshots from the Bill Thorn Gala

COACHING ACCOLADES

OVERALL

Hall of Fame Awards: 4

Coach of the Year Awards: 131

State championship teams: 42

Individual state champions (including relay teams): 173

COACH OF THE YEAR AWARDS

Football:

GHSA Region (1967-1968), AISA State (1991)

Boys' Track:

Atlanta Track Club—GHSA

(1996, 1997, 1998, 1999, 2000, 2001, 2008, 2016, 2019)

Region—GHSA

(1963, 1964, 1967, 1969, 1993, 1994, 1995, 1996, 1997, 1998, 1999, 2000, 2001, 2002, 2003, 2004, 2008, 2013, 2015, 2016, 2017, 2018, 2019)

State—GHSA

(1996, 1997, 1998, 1999, 2000, 2002, 2008, 2016, 2019)

Girls' Track:

Atlanta Track Club—GHSA

(2000, 2001, 2002, 2003, 2004, 2005, 2008)

Region—GHSA

(2001, 2002, 2003, 2004, 2005, 2008, 2016, 2017, 2018)

State—GHSA

(2000, 2001, 2002, 2003, 2004, 2005, 2008)

Boys' Cross-Country:
Atlanta Track Club—GHSA
(1999, 2000, 2002, 2003, 2004, 2013, 2015, 2016)
Region—GHSA
(1999, 2000, 2001, 2002, 2004, 2005, 2013, 2015, 2016, 2017)
State—GHSA
(1999, 2000, 2002, 2003, 2004, 2013, 2015, 2016)

Girls' Cross-Country:
Atlanta Track Club—GHSA
(2003, 2004, 2005, 2006, 2007, 2011, 2012, 2014, 2015, 2016, 2017)
Region—GHSA
(2000, 2001, 2002, 2003, 2004, 2005, 2006, 2007, 2012, 2014, 2015, 2016, 2017)
State—GHSA
(1999, 2000, 2002, 2003, 2004, 2013, 2014, 2015, 2016, 2017)

Bill with his collection of championship patches, rings, and watches

RECORDS BY SPORT

Football—26 Years Head Coach

Overall record: 186-84-5

State championships: 3

State runner-up titles: 3

Regional championships: 3

Girls' Cross-Country—20 Years Head Coach

State championships: 11

State runner-up titles: 1

Regional championships: 13

Boys' Cross-Country—20 Years Head Coach

State championships: 8

State runner-up titles: 4

Regional championships: 10

Girls' Track—20 Years Head Coach

State championships: 7

State runner-up titles: 3

Regional championships: 9

Boys' Track—45 Years Head Coach

State championships: 13

State runner-up titles: 9

Regional championships: 22

LIST OF CHAMPIONSHIP TEAMS						
Year	Sport	School	Regional Champion	State Runner-Up	State Champion	Governing Authority
1963	Boys' Track	Headland	X			GHSA
1964	Boys' Track	Headland	X	X		GHSA
1967	Football	Headland	X			GHSA
1967	Boys' Track	Headland	X			GHSA
1968	Football	Headland	X			GHSA
1969	Boys' Track	Headland	X	X		GHSA
1982	Football	Colonial Hills			X	GACA
1982	Boys' Track	Colonial Hills			X	GACA
1983	Boys' Track	Colonial Hills			X	GACA
1984	Boys' Track	Colonial Hills		X		PCAC
1984	Football	Colonial Hills			X	PCAC
1985	Football	Colonial Hills		X		SCAC
1985	Boys' Track	Colonial Hills		X		SCAC
1987	Football	Fayette Christian		X		GACA
1988	Football	Fayette Christian			X	SCAC
1991	Boys' Track	Landmark			X	AISA
1991	Football	Landmark		X		AISA
1992	Boys' Track	Landmark		X		AISA
1993	Boys' Track	Landmark	X			GHSA
1994	Boys' Track	Landmark	X			GHSA
1995	Boys' Track	Landmark	X	X		GHSA
1996	Boys' Track	Landmark	X		X	GHSA

LIST OF CHAMPIONSHIP TEAMS						
Year	Sport	School	Regional Champion	State Runner-Up	State Champion	Governing Authority
1997	Boys' Track	Landmark	X		X	GHSA
1998	Boys' Track	Landmark	X		X	GHSA
1999	Boys' XC	Landmark	X		X	GHSA
1999	Boys' Track	Landmark	X		X	GHSA
2000	Girls' Track	Landmark			X	GHSA
2000	Boys' XC	Landmark	X		X	GHSA
2000	Girls' XC	Landmark	X			GHSA
2000	Boys' Track	Landmark	X		X	GHSA
2001	Boys' XC	Landmark	X	X		GHSA
2001	Girls' XC	Landmark	X			GHSA
2001	Boys' Track	Landmark	X		X	GHSA
2001	Girls' Track	Landmark	X		X	GHSA
2002	Boys' XC	Landmark	X		X	GHSA
2002	Girls' XC	Landmark	X	X		GHSA
2002	Boys' Track	Landmark	X		X	GHSA
2002	Girls' Track	Landmark	X		X	GHSA
2003	Girls' XC	Landmark	X		X	GHSA
2003	Boys' Track	Landmark	X	X		GHSA
2003	Boys' XC	Landmark			X	GHSA
2003	Girls' Track	Landmark	X		X	GHSA
2004	Boys' XC	Landmark	X		X	GHSA
2004	Girls' XC	Landmark	X		X	GHSA
2004	Boys' Track	Landmark	X			GHSA
2004	Girls' Track	Landmark	X		X	GHSA
2005	Boys' XC	Landmark	X	X		GHSA
2005	Girls' XC	Landmark	X		X	GHSA
2005	Girls' Track	Landmark	X		X	GHSA

LIST OF CHAMPIONSHIP TEAMS						
Year	Sport	School	Regional Champion	State Runner-Up	State Champion	Governing Authority
2006	Girls' Track	Landmark		X		GHSA
2006	Boys' XC	Landmark		X		GHSA
2006	Girls' XC	Landmark	X		X	GHSA
2007	Girls' Track	Landmark		X		GHSA
2007	Girls' XC	Landmark	X		X	GHSA
2008	Boys' Track	Landmark	X		X	GHSA
2008	Girls' Track	Landmark	X		X	GHSA
2011	Girls' XC	Landmark			X	GHSA
2012	Girls' XC	Landmark	X		X	GHSA
2013	Boys' Track	Landmark	X	X		GHSA
2013	Boys' XC	Landmark	X		X	GHSA
2014	Girls' Track	Landmark		X		GHSA
2014	Girls' XC	Landmark	X		X	GHSA
2015	Boys' Track	Landmark	X			GHSA
2015	Boys' XC	Landmark	X		X	GHSA
2015	Girls' XC	Landmark	X		X	GHSA
2016	Boys' Track	Landmark	X		X	GHSA
2016	Girls' Track	Landmark	X			GHSA
2016	Boys' XC	Landmark	X		X	GHSA
2016	Girls' XC	Landmark	X		X	GHSA
2017	Girls' Track	Landmark	X			GHSA
2017	Boys' XC	Landmark	X	X		GHSA
2017	Boys' Track	Landmark		X		GHSA
2017	Girls' XC	Landmark	X		X	GHSA
2018	Boys' Track	Landmark	X			GHSA
2018	Girls' Track	Landmark	X			GHSA
2019	Boys' Track	Landmark	X		X	GHSA

SCAC: Southern Christian Athletic Conference
AISA: Alabama Independent School Association
PCAC: Peach State Conference
GACA: Georgia Athletic Christian Association
GHSA: Georgia High School Association

COACH THORN'S INDIVIDUAL FOOTBALL GAME RECORDS AS HEAD COACH*

Type Key: R-Regular Season Game, P-Playoff Game, C-Championship Game, NR-Score Not Recorded, F-Forfeit

Year	School	Opponent	School	Opponent	Result	Type
1961	Headland	Hapeville	12	0	W	R
1961	Headland	College Park	13	12	W	R
1961	Headland	North Clayton	20	18	W	R
1961	Headland	Newnan	6	14	L	R
1961	Headland	Campbell	6	27	L	R
1961	Headland	Milton	28	6	W	R
1961	Headland	Douglas Co	0	8	L	R
1961	Headland	Westminster	0	34	L	R
1961	Headland	Forest Park	20	27	L	R
1961	Headland	Sandy Springs	12	24	L	R
1962	Headland	College Park	14	7	W	R
1962	Headland	Douglas Co	14	13	W	R
1962	Headland	Hapeville	21	0	W	R
1962	Headland	Campbell	0	7	L	R
1962	Headland	Milton	49	6	W	R
1962	Headland	Newnan	7	0	W	R
1962	Headland	Osborne	18	3	W	R

*Data sourced from Coach Thorn's personal records and school yearbooks, as well as the Georgia High School Football History database.

1962	Headland	Lakeshore	20	0	W	R
1962	Headland	Sandy Springs	7	0	W	R
1962	Headland	Jonesboro	20	6	W	R
1962	Headland	North Clayton	6	18	L	P
1963	Headland	College Park	14	14	T	R
1963	Headland	Douglas Co	26	12	W	R
1963	Headland	Hapeville	21	0	W	R
1963	Headland	Campbell	14	0	W	R
1963	Headland	Milton	33	7	W	R
1963	Headland	Newnan	26	6	W	R
1963	Headland	Osborne	14	21	L	R
1963	Headland	Lakeshore	25	0	W	R
1963	Headland	Sandy Springs	21	0	W	R
1963	Headland	Jonesboro	25	3	W	R
1963	Headland	College Park	0	14	L	P
1964	Headland	Russell	15	12	W	R
1964	Headland	Troup	21	0	W	R
1964	Headland	Therrell	14	3	W	R
1964	Headland	Campbell	33	13	W	R
1964	Headland	Douglas Co	6	6	L	R
1964	Headland	Sandy Springs	7	0	W	R
1964	Headland	Hapeville	21	0	W	R
1964	Headland	Lakeshore	27	7	W	R
1964	Headland	St. Pius X	10	0	W	R
1964	Headland	College Park	7	6	W	R
1964	Headland	Douglas Co	13	16	L	P
1965	Headland	Russell	19	7	W	R
1965	Headland	Troup	19	0	W	R
1965	Headland	Therrell	19	0	W	R
1965	Headland	Campbell	0	7	L	R

1965	Headland	Douglas Co	7	13	L	R
1965	Headland	Sandy Springs	14	34	L	R
1965	Headland	Hapeville	20	0	W	R
1965	Headland	Lakeshore	20	12	W	R
1965	Headland	St. Pius X	0	13	L	R
1965	Headland	College Park	7	3	W	R
1966	Headland	Woodward	0	6	L	R
1966	Headland	Russell	17	0	W	R
1966	Headland	Troup	36	0	W	R
1966	Headland	Campbell	3	0	W	R
1966	Headland	Douglas Co	23	13	W	R
1966	Headland	Newnan	6	21	L	R
1966	Headland	North Clayton	41	14	W	R
1966	Headland	Lakeshore	0	0	T	R
1966	Headland	Hapeville	7	6	W	R
1966	Headland	College Park	14	6	W	R
1967	Headland	Woodward	0	20	L	R
1967	Headland	Russell	19	6	W	R
1967	Headland	Troup	19	6	W	R
1967	Headland	Campbell	12	7	W	R
1967	Headland	Douglas Co	14	6	W	R
1967	Headland	Newnan	0	20	L	R
1967	Headland	North Clayton	19	9	W	R
1967	Headland	Lakeshore	28	7	W	R
1967	Headland	Hapeville	21	13	W	R
1967	Headland	College Park	20	6	W	R
1967	Headland	Carver	14	19	L	P
1968	Headland	LaGrange	19	19	T	R
1968	Headland	Campbell	14	6	W	R
1968	Headland	Troup	34	13	W	R

1968	Headland	Russell	20	7	W	R
1968	Headland	Lakeshore	7	14	L	R
1968	Headland	Hapeville	34	0	W	R
1968	Headland	South Fulton	23	0	W	R
1968	Headland	Briarwood	43	0	W	R
1968	Headland	College Park	21	13	W	R
1968	Headland	Lakeview-Ft. Oglethorpe	39	0	W	R
1968	Headland	Lakeshore	14	10	W	P
1968	Headland	Thomasville	7	10	L	P
1981	CHCS	Gilead	0	6	L	R
1981	CHCS	Forrest Hills	12	8	W	R
1981	CHCS	Donelson	6	0	W	R
1981	CHCS	Central Fellowship	21	6	W	R
1981	CHCS	Mount Vernon	6	19	L	R
1981	CHCS	Marietta	0	18	L	R
1981	CHCS	Lake City	20	26	L	R
1981	CHCS	Athens	0	14	L	R
1982	CHCS	Forrest Hills	12	12	T	R
1982	CHCS	Lake City	26	12	W	R
1982	CHCS	Forest Park	6	7	L	R
1982	CHCS	Central Fellowship	40	0	W	R
1982	CHCS	Mount Vernon	27	6	W	R
1982	CHCS	King's Way	35	0	W	R
1982	CHCS	Chapel Hill	29	3	W	R
1982	CHCS	Marietta	25	0	W	R
1982	CHCS	Chapel Hill	38	13	W	R
1982	CHCS	Athens	27	0	W	R
1982	CHCS	Forest Park	26	6	W	P

1982	CHCS	Athens	7	6	W	C
1983	CHCS	Coosa	34	14	W	R
1983	CHCS	Anneewakee	18	16	W	R
1983	CHCS	Central Fellowship	24	0	W	R
1983	CHCS	Mount Vernon	45	6	W	R
1983	CHCS	Chapel Hill	39	0	W	R
1983	CHCS	Fullington	28	16	W	R
1983	CHCS	Calvary	14	0	W	R
1983	CHCS	Shiloh Hills	24	12	W	R
1983	CHCS	Marietta	30	0	W	R
1983	CHCS	Maranatha	14	21	L	R
1984	CHCS	Forrest Hills	22	0	W	R
1984	CHCS	Coosa	14	8	W	R
1984	CHCS	Maranatha	49	0	W	R
1984	CHCS	Mount Vernon	22	0	W	R
1984	CHCS	Pineland	27	20	W	R
1984	CHCS	Chapel Hill	21	0	W	R
1984	CHCS	Shiloh Hills	27	12	W	R
1984	CHCS	Calvary	27	0	W	R
1984	CHCS	Westminster	20	23	L	R
1984	CHCS	Coosa	8	15	L	P
1984	CHCS	Bethlehem	0	16	L	P
1984	CHCS	Bible Baptist	34	14	W	C
1985	CHCS	Coosa	14	6	W	R
1985	CHCS	Gilead	27	0	W	R
1985	CHCS	Pineland	32	6	W	R
1985	CHCS	One Way	60	0	W	R
1985	CHCS	Mount Vernon	26	0	W	R
1985	CHCS	Athens	49	0	W	R

1985	CHCS	Calvary	25	0	W	R
1985	CHCS	Forrest Hills	46	0	W	R
1985	CHCS	Westminster	24	6	W	R
1985	CHCS	Cathedral	32	12	W	R
1985	CHCS	Independent Methodist	14	31	L	C
1986	CHCS	Panama City	20	0	W	R
1986	CHCS	Hammond	28	6	W	R
1986	CHCS	Shiloh Hills	35	14	W	R
1986	CHCS	Coosa	53	41	W	R
1986	CHCS	Shiloh Hills	95	47	W	R
1986	CHCS	Lake City	6	9	L	R
1986	CHCS	Coosa	21	27	L	R
1986	CHCS	Westbrook	14	21	L	R
1986	CHCS	West Birmingham	42	6	W	R
1987	Fayette Christian	Central Fellowship	NR	NR	W	R
1987	Fayette Christian	Colonial Hills	NR	NR	W	R
1987	Fayette Christian	Maranatha	NR	NR	W	R
1987	Fayette Christian	Pineland	NR	NR	W	R
1987	Fayette Christian	Gilead	NR	NR	L	R
1987	Fayette Christian	Gilead	8	28	L	P
1987	Fayette Christian	Coosa	7	13	L	R
1987	Fayette Christian	West Birmingham	7	47	L	R
1987	Fayette Christian	Athens	0	49	L	R
1987	Fayette Christian	Tuscaloosa	20	14	W	R
1988	Fayette Christian	Athens	28	33	L	R
1988	Fayette Christian	Cathedral	46	0	W	R
1988	Fayette Christian	Coosa	34	22	W	R

1988	Fayette Christian	Colonial Hills	26	6	W	R
1988	Fayette Christian	Mount Vernon	32	20	W	R
1988	Fayette Christian	Gilead	44	31	W	R
1988	Fayette Christian	Pineland	38	0	W	R
1988	Fayette Christian	West Birmingham	20	12	W	R
1988	Fayette Christian	Tuscaloosa	26	6	W	R
1988	Fayette Christian	Westminster	13	0	W	C
1989	Landmark Christian	King's Way	NR	NR	W	R
1989	Landmark Christian	LaGrange	NR	NR	W	R
1989	Landmark Christian	Lake City	NR	NR	W	R
1989	Landmark Christian	Mount Vernon	NR	NR	W	R
1989	Landmark Christian	Shiloh Hills	NR	NR	W	R
1989	Landmark Christian	American	8	22	L	R
1989	Landmark Christian	George Walton	0	35	L	R
1989	Landmark Christian	Athens	7	12	L	R
1989	Landmark Christian	West Birmingham	NR	NR	W	R
1989	Landmark Christian	Tuscaloosa	44	0	W	R
1990	Landmark Christian	Shiloh Hills	34	6	W	R
1990	Landmark Christian	Athens	7	6	W	R
1990	Landmark Christian	Lake City	41	13	W	R
1990	Landmark Christian	Chambers	22	25	L	R

1990	Landmark Christian	Pike	42	24	W	R
1990	Landmark Christian	Mount Vernon	37	6	W	R
1990	Landmark Christian	Edgewood	25	0	W	R
1990	Landmark Christian	Glenwood	0	3	L	R
1990	Landmark Christian	Lakeside	34	18	W	R
1990	Landmark Christian	Lee-Scott	20	12	W	R
1990	Landmark Christian	Wilcox	21	7	W	P
1990	Landmark Christian	Glenwood	12	28	L	P
1991	Landmark Christian	Piedmont	20	0	W	R
1991	Landmark Christian	LaGrange	28	12	W	R
1991	Landmark Christian	Athens	30	21	W	R
1991	Landmark Christian	Shiloh Hills	28	0	W	R
1991	Landmark Christian	Pike	14	6	W	R
1991	Landmark Christian	Chambers	52	19	W	R
1991	Landmark Christian	Edgewood	32	0	W	R
1991	Landmark Christian	Glenwood	22	29	L	R
1991	Landmark Christian	Rutledge	N/A	F	W	R
1991	Landmark Christian	Lakeside	6	18	L	R

1991	Landmark Christian	Lee-Scott	34	18	W	R
1991	Landmark Christian	Sumter	19	0	W	P
1991	Landmark Christian	Patrician	6	0	W	P
1991	Landmark Christian	Glenwood	12	30	L	C
1992	Landmark Christian	Jordan	7	21	L	R
1992	Landmark Christian	Hayesville	12	17	L	R
1992	Landmark Christian	Riverside	32	7	W	R
1992	Landmark Christian	Salem	39	6	W	R
1992	Landmark Christian	Mount Zion	8	0	W	R
1992	Landmark Christian	Greater Atlanta	36	19	W	R
1992	Landmark Christian	Chamblee	22	0	W	R
1992	Landmark Christian	East Paulding	6	6	T	R
1992	Landmark Christian	Decatur	6	19	L	R
1992	Landmark Christian	Temple	38	0	W	R
1992	Landmark Christian	Mount Zion	14	18	L	P
1993	Landmark Christian	Jordan	7	21	L	R
1993	Landmark Christian	Hayesville	14	26	L	R
1993	Landmark Christian	Riverside	35	14	W	R

1993	Landmark Christian	Salem	33	13	W	R
1993	Landmark Christian	Mount Zion	14	17	L	R
1993	Landmark Christian	Greater Atlanta	40	8	W	R
1993	Landmark Christian	Chamblee	34	0	W	R
1993	Landmark Christian	East Paulding	0	47	L	R
1993	Landmark Christian	Decatur	0	24	L	R
1993	Landmark Christian	Temple	25	14	W	R
1993	Landmark Christian	Mount Zion	41	13	W	P
1993	Landmark Christian	Armuchee	13	35	L	P
1994	Landmark Christian	Georgia Military	21	0	W	R
1994	Landmark Christian	Brookstone	26	2	W	R
1994	Landmark Christian	Towns Co	13	0	W	R
1994	Landmark Christian	Douglass	34	0	W	R
1994	Landmark Christian	Mount Zion	7	21	L	R
1994	Landmark Christian	Bowdon	23	30	L	R
1994	Landmark Christian	Greater Atlanta	8	21	L	R
1994	Landmark Christian	Breman	28	36	L	R
1994	Landmark Christian	Temple	8	24	L	R

1994	Landmark Christian	Decatur	18	55	L	R
1995	Landmark Christian	Georgia Military	17	0	W	R
1995	Landmark Christian	Brookstone	8	22	L	R
1995	Landmark Christian	Towns Co	32	6	W	R
1995	Landmark Christian	Douglass	21	14	W	R
1995	Landmark Christian	Mount Zion	14	38	L	R
1995	Landmark Christian	Bowdon	26	54	L	R
1995	Landmark Christian	Greater Atlanta	20	28	L	R
1995	Landmark Christian	Bremen	7	18	L	R
1995	Landmark Christian	Temple	8	26	L	R
1995	Landmark Christian	Decatur	13	40	L	R
1996	Landmark Christian	Brookstone	18	21	L	R
1996	Landmark Christian	Model	0	28	L	R
1996	Landmark Christian	Oglethorpe Co	28	21	W	R
1996	Landmark Christian	Madison	26	0	W	R
1996	Landmark Christian	Mount Zion	3	10	L	R
1996	Landmark Christian	Bowdon	12	18	L	R
1996	Landmark Christian	Greater Atlanta	8	27	L	R

1996	Landmark Christian	Bremen	8	27	L	R
1996	Landmark Christian	Temple	36	6	W	R
1996	Landmark Christian	Decatur	35	28	W	R
1997	Landmark Christian	Brookstone	31	14	W	R
1997	Landmark Christian	Model	13	6	W	R
1997	Landmark Christian	Oglethorpe Co	19	14	W	R
1997	Landmark Christian	Madison	42	6	W	R
1997	Landmark Christian	Mount Zion	34	0	W	R
1997	Landmark Christian	Bowdon	42	21	W	R
1997	Landmark Christian	Greater Atlanta	14	28	L	R
1997	Landmark Christian	Bremen	54	24	W	R
1997	Landmark Christian	Temple	12	0	W	R
1997	Landmark Christian	Decatur	46	22	W	R
1997	Landmark Christian	Model	27	6	W	P
1997	Landmark Christian	Commerce	0	27	L	P
1998	Landmark Christian	Greater Atlanta	15	41	L	R
1998	Landmark Christian	Lovett	0	21	L	R
1998	Landmark Christian	Heard Co	21	20	W	R

1998	Landmark Christian	Callaway	21	6	W	R
1998	Landmark Christian	Northgate	38	14	W	R
1998	Landmark Christian	Bremen	28	31	L	R
1998	Landmark Christian	Temple	35	40	L	R
1998	Landmark Christian	Mount Zion	48	0	W	R
1998	Landmark Christian	Greenville	7	32	L	R
1998	Landmark Christian	Bowdon	0	42	L	R

TRACK AND FIELD RECORDS*

GIRLS' TRACK AND FIELD CHAMPIONS

Year	Athlete	Event
1999	Terria Curtis, Celeste Lee, Trisia Van Wout, Rashedah Arnold	4x400 Relay
2000	Lindsey Vincent	400
2001	Sierra Hill, Rashedah Arnold, Ashley Key, Sarah King	4x100 Relay
2001	Sarah King	400
2001	Rashedah Arnold	100
2001	Sierra Hill	100H
2001	Rashedah Arnold	200
2001	Sierra Hill	300H
2001	Emily Wood	3200
2001	Sarah King, Ashley Key, Kathryn Wright, Sierra Hill	4x400 Relay
2001	Ashley Key	High Jump
2001	Lindsey Vincent	Long Jump
2002	Lindsey Vincent	400
2002	Rashedah Arnold	100
2002	Sierra Hill	100H
2002	Rashedah Arnold	200
2002	Sierra Hill	300H
2002	Sarah King, Evette Holyfield, Sierra Hill, Lindsey Vincent	4x400 Relay
2002	Lindsey Vincent	Triple Jump
2002	Lindsey Vincent	Long Jump
2002	Kristina Eden	1600
2002	Sierra Hill, Sarah King, Lindsey Vincent, Rashedah Arnold	4x100 Relay
2003	Sierra Hill, Sarah King, Evette Holyfield, Kristina Eden	4x100 Relay
2003	Evette Holyfield	400
2003	Sierra Hill	100H

*Data sourced from Bill's personal records, as well as the databases provided by the Georgia Track & Field/Cross Country Coaches Association (GATFXCCA).

Year	Athlete	Event
2003	Evette Holyfield	200
2003	Sierra Hill	300H
2003	Sierra Hill, Sarah King, Evette Holyfield, Lynette Fitts	4x400 Relay
2003	Sarah King	Pole Vault
2003	Lindsey Vincent	Long Jump
2004	Ciara Willis, Evette Holyfield, Lynette Fitts, Sierra Hill	4x100 Relay*
2004	Ciara Willis	400
2004	Sierra Hill	100H*
2004	Ciara Willis	200
2004	Sierra Hill	300H*
2004	Ciara Willis, Evette Holyfield, Lynette Fitts, Sierra Hill	4x400 Relay*
2004	Heather Hayes	Pole Vault
2004	Evette Holyfield	Triple Jump
2005	Heather Hayes, Ciara Willis, Kaity Bulger, Christian McGuire	4x400 Relay
2005	Ciara Willis	4x400 Relay
2005	Kaity Bulger	4x400 Relay
2005	Christian McGuire	4x400 Relay

Year	Athlete	Event
2005	Heather Hayes	Pole Vault
2005	Ciara Willis	200
2006	Heather Hayes	300H
2006	Kelsey Knapp, Heather Hayes, Christian McGuire, Kaity Bulger	4x400 Relay
2007	Kaity Bulger	800
2007	Christian McGuire	300H
2007	Christian McGuire	100H
2007	Kaity Bulger	Pole Vault
2008	Kaity Bulger, Christian McGuire, Lauren Toomer, Alysa Rambo	4x400 Relay
2008	Christian McGuire	110H
2008	Christian McGuire	300H
2010	Lindy Long	3200
2010	Lauren Toomer	100H
2011	Lindy Long	3200
2013	Lindy Long	3200
2017	Nicole Fegans	3200
2017	Nicole Fegans	1600
2018	Elizabeth Gibbs	Discus
2018	Erin Fegans	3200
2019	Erin Fegans	3200

** Current Georgia "Private (A)" state record (as of 2025)*

BOYS' TRACK AND FIELD CHAMPIONS

Year	Athlete	Event
1969	Mark Brown	1600
1995	Matt Day	1600
1995	Evan McNary	3200
1995	Brannon Duncan	400
1995	Matt Day	800
1996	Matt Day	1600
1996	Tim McNary	3200
1996	Brannon Duncan	400
1996	Matt Day	800
1997	Matt Day	1600
1997	Matt Day	800
1998	Kyle Rabbitt	800
1999	Kyle Rabbitt	800
1999	Nathan Koshiba	3200
1999	Kyle Rabbitt	1600
1999	Joseph Cawood	Pole Vault
1999	Eric Quint, Nick Polgardi, Chris Rentz, Ken Harris	4x400 Relay
2000	Kyle Rabbitt	1600
2000	Nathan Koshiba	3200
2000	Eric Quint	Pole Vault
2000	Sean Hill, Eric Quint, Nick Polgardi, Chris Rentz	4x400 Relay
2000	Brady Rockmore	Triple Jump
2001	Clark Rivers	1600
2001	Clark Rivers	3200
2001	Joseph Register	Pole Vault
2001	Brady Rockmore	Triple Jump
2002	Clark Rivers	1600
2002	Blake Fertitta	3200
2002	Brady Rockmore	Triple Jump
2003	Sean Hill	300H
2003	Blake Fertitta	3200
2003	Joseph Register	Pole Vault
2004	Will Bonn	1600
2004	Will Bonn	3200
2004	Adam Lewis	Pole Vault
2005	Will Bonn	1600
2005	Will Bonn	3200
2006	Chad Thames	3200
2008	Walter Lenard	110H
2008	Durrell Smith	300H
2009	Marlon Bryan	100H
2009	Marlon Bryan	300H
2013	Cole Higbie, Austin Hoover, Stockton McGuire, Darius Smith	4x400 Relay
2016	Drew Anderson	Discus
2017	Nicolas Toomer	Triple Jump
2017	Brandon Stone	300H
2017	Donovan Pickett, Kermit Jackson, Brandon Stone, Nicolas Toomer	4x400 Relay
2018	Zack Truitt	3200
2019	Zack Truitt	1600
2019	Kameron Jackson	800
2019	Tyler Spann, Zack Truitt, Omari Hammond, Kameron Jackson	4x400 Relay

INDIVIDUAL GIRLS' CROSS-COUNTRY CHAMPIONS

Year	Athlete
2009	Lindy Long
2012	Kathryn Foreman
2013	Kathryn Foreman
2016	Nicole Fegans
2017	Mary Kellison Thorne

INDIVIDUAL BOYS' CROSS-COUNTRY CHAMPIONS

Year	Athlete
1999	Kyle Rabbitt
2002	Blake Fertitta
2004	Will Bonn
2016	Seth Cruver

CHAMPIONSHIP PHOTOS

1982 Colonial Hills Football

Claude Brown, Mark Green, Hal Calhoun, Rodney Brooks, David Stewart, Phil Carlson, John Selfe, David Wilkins, Larry West, John Bass, Larry Amburgey, Jeff Doris, Jeff Alexander, Sean Brown, Mark Payne, James Murphy, Todd Calhoun

1982 Colonial Hills Boys' Track

1983 Colonial Hills Boys' Track

1984 Colonial Hills Football

Jeff Alexander, Greg Tankersly, Brian Todd, John Selfe, Conn Barrow, Jay Hudson, Donald Brooks, Skeeter Stacks, Tim Plemmons, Brian Pierce, Eric Dial, Parrish Walker, Lynn Smithwick, David Kite, Murice Miller, Joe Steward, Jeff Hood, Brian Hopkins, Richie Lankford, Casey Copeland, Jody Yancey, Todd Calhoun, Dee Claborn, Chuck Eidson, Jeff Law, Craig Page

1988 Fayette Christian Football

1991 LCS Boys' Track and Field

1996 LCS Boys' Track and Field

Tim McNary, Nathan Lee, Andrew Cathy, Matt Day, Lance Batiste, Shane Odom, Ben Stout, Brannon Duncan, John Harkey, Adam Hanes, Matt Jarrett, Kevin Rogers, Jonathan Sumner, Matt Underwood, David Cox

1997 LCS Boys' Track and Field

Tim McNary, Nathan Kosiba, Jeremiah Register, Andrew Cathy, Joseph Cawood, Adam Hanes, Matt Underwood, Chris Fears, Josh Bruner, John Harkey, Ken Harris, CaBrandon Johnson, Kyle Whitson, Terrance Penn, Jonathan Book, Kevin Rogers, Jonathan Sumner, Ben Stout, Matt Jarrett, Joe Stephens, Nick Polgardi, Hayes Mercure, Lance Batiste

1998 LCS Boys' Track and Field

Jeremiah Register, Hayes Mercure, Lance Batiste, Nick Polgardi, Joe Stephens, Ken Harris, Ben Stout, Chris Rentz, Jordan Baldwin, Jeremy Ragsdale, Nathan Welden, Kyle Rabbitt, Nathan Kosiba, Jonathan Sumner, Adam Hanes

LANDMARK
CHRISTIAN SCHOOL

1999 LCS Boys' Cross-Country

Kyle Rabbitt, Nathan Kosiba, Clark Rivers, Blake Fertitta, Eric Sumner, Jonathan Best, Chris Rogers

1999 LCS Boys' Track and Field

Clark Rivers, Chris Rogers, Chris Ireland, James Emanuel, Marvin Jinks, Nathan Kosiba, Eric Quint, Joseph Cawood, Jeff Noble, Jonathan Sumner, Taylor Brooks, Ken Harris, Jordan Baldwin, Ben King, Kyle Rabbitt, Tim Fritz, Darren Lee, Nathan Williams, CaBrandon Johnson, Nick Polgardi, Michael Watson, Joe Stephens, Hayes Mercure, Terrance Penn, Ray Ross, Chris Rentz

2000 LCS Girls' Track and Field

Megan Constable, Layla Constable, Lindsey Vincent, Rashedah Arnold, Lindsey Huether, Melissa Register, Courtney Piribek

2000 LCS Boys' Cross-Country
Jeff Noble, Scott Emery, Blake Fertitta, Clark Rivers, Alan Gay, Eric Sumner, Joseph Register, Jonathan Best, Dustin McDonald, Matt Coffey, Tim Fritz

2000 LCS Boys' Track and Field
Ben King, Chris Ireland, Blake Fertitta, Chris Rentz, Joseph Cawood, Kyle Rabbitt, Nathan Kosiba, Eric Sumner, Nick Polgardi, Sean Hill, Eric Quint

2001 LCS Boys' Track and Field
Jeff Noble, Eric Sumner, Clark Rivers, Eric Worrell, James Emanuel, Joseph Register, Sean Hill, Tim Fritz, Blake Fertitta, Alan Gay, Michael Fritz, Dustin McDonald, Brady Rockmore, Todd Moret, Jordan Baldwin, Darren Lee, Adam Lewis, Ben King, Benjamin Cawood

2001 LCS Girls' Track and Field
Katie Bailey, Sarah King, Danielle Taussig, Emily Wood, Sierra Hill, Megan Constable, Andrea Wooding, Layla Constable, Rashedah Arnold, Mary Michael Joiner, Erica Bulger, Melissa Register, Lindsey Vincent, Holly Hurst, Joy Huether, Courtney Piribek, Ashley Key, Katherine Wright, Morgan Mozley

2002 LCS Boys' Cross-Country
Blake Fertitta, Robert Jones, James Register, Will Bonn, Joseph Register, Dustin McDonald, Michael Fritz

2002 LCS Boys' Track and Field
Clark Rivers, Ben King, Brady Rockmore, Chris Ireland, Eric Sumner, Sean Hill, Tory Roberson, Evander Holyfield, Joseph Register, Blake Fertitta, Bobby Weaver, John David Houston

2002 LCS Girls' Track and Field
Sierra Hill, Courtney Piribek, Kate Bailey, Emily Wood, Mary Michael Joiner, Ashley Brown, Kristina Eden, Evette Holyfield, Lindsey Vincent, Sarah King, Rasheda Arnold

2003 LCS Girls' Cross-Country
Mary Michael Joiner, Christina Vera, Caroline Jones, Sarah King, Nia Baker, Sarah Blanton, Kristina Eden, Hope Hurst, Emily Wood, Jesse Tahmes

2003 LCS Boys' Cross-Country
Robert Jones, Will Bonn, Brett Lewis, Bobby Weaver, Michael Fritz, Jacob Parker, Bradley Eisenburg

2003 LCS Girls' Track and Field
Evette Holyfield, Sierra Hill, Sarah King, Kristina Eden, Lindsey Vincent, Emily Wood, Lynette Fitts, Jessie Thames

2004 LCS Boys' Cross-Country
Brett Lewis, Will Bonn, Zack Speir, Bradley Eisenburg, Michael Leonard, Chad Thames, Alec Pike, Darin Branton

2004 LCS Girls' Cross-Country
Jesse Tahmes, Kassi Deel, Sarah Blanton, Caroline Jones, Kaity Bulger, Erin Kelly

2004 LCS Girls' Track and Field
Ciara Willis, Jessica Vautin, Janell Henderson, Ebonne Holyfield, Evette Holyfield, Sarah King, Lynette Fitts, Heather Hayes, Kristina Eden, Sierra Hill

2005 LCS Girls' Cross-Country
Kaity Bulger, Elizabeth Gresham, Christian McGuire, Kassi Deel, Caroline Jones, Jesse Tahmes, Lauren McGuire

2005 LCS Girls' Track and Field
Christian McGuire, Ciara Willis, Jesse Tahmes, Kaity Bulger, Heather Hayes, Lynette Fitts, Evette Holyfield, Sarah Blanton, Ebonne Holyfield

2006 LCS Girls' Cross-Country
Erin Hogan, Christian McGuire, Kaity Bulger, Lauren McGuire, Caroline Jones, Amy Stuart, Janie Parker, Jesse Thames, Elizabeth Gresham, Kassi Deel

2007 LCS Girls' Cross-Country
Hannah Gravitt, Kenzie Thrasher, Georgiana Moody, Kassi Deel, Christian McGuire, Kaley Cusumano, Kaity Bulger, Kathleen Duncan

2008 LCS Boys' Track and Field
Durrell Smith, Chad Thames, Marlon Bryan, Austin Broussard, Andrew Glaize, Greg Powell, Blake Wyatt, Walter Lenard

2008 LCS Girls' Track and Field
Hannah Gravitt, Alysa Rambo, Kenzie Thrasher, Lauren Toomer, Kaity Bulger, Joel Christian, Kathleen Duncan, Alex Glaize, Christian McGuire, Erin Kelly

2011 LCS Girls' Cross-Country
Lana Hojeij, Kaylin Deel, Abby Glaize, Kaley Cusumano, Karis Stuker, Kensi Deel, Lindy Long, Hannah Hankins

2012 LCS Girls' Cross-Country
Kathryn Foreman, Lindy Long, Rachel Morley, Courtney Gilliam, Kaylin Deel, Taylor Biggar, Rebecca Moody

2013 LCS Boys' Cross-Country
Spencer Geerlings, Taylor Austin, Brandon Regan, Joe Humphries, Daniel Wilson, Ty Janyaem, Seth Cruver

2014 LCS Girls' Cross-Country
Nicole Fegans, Kathryn Foreman, Sarah Foreman, Mary Kellison Thorne, Lindsey Biggar, Courtney Gilliam, Taylor Biggar

2015 LCS Boys' Cross-Country
Seth Cruver, Austin Taylor, Daniel Wilson, Micah Burdette, Mark Humphries, Colton Wooster, Jack Drury

2015 LCS Girls' Cross-Country
Nicole Fegans, Kathryn Foreman, Mary Kellison Thorne, Sarah Foreman, Lindsey Biggar, Madison Schmidlkofer, Taylor Biggar

2016 LCS Boys' Track and Field
Nicolas Toomer, Taylor Snyder, Kermit Jackson, Seth Cruver, Brandon Stone, Stockton McGuire, Caleb Cobb, Drew Anderson

2016 LCS Boys' Cross-Country
Seth Cruver, Kermit Jackson, Kameron Jackson, Jack Drury, Mark Humphries, Colton Wooster, Micah Burdette

2016 LCS Girls' Cross-Country
Lindsey Biggar, Sarah Foreman, Madison Schmidlkofer, Mary Kellison Thorne, Kathryn Foreman, Nicole Fegans, Taylor Biggar

2017 LCS Girls' Cross-Country
Mary Kellison Thorne, Erin Fegans, Sarah Foreman, Lindsey Biggar, Jenny Goodwin, Anna Butler

2019 LCS Boys' Track and Field
Andy Cruver, Braxton Brown, Joshua Smith, Micah McAllister, Brogan Korta, Joshua Smith, Zack Truitt, Kameron Jackson, Omari Hammond, Tyler Spann

INDEX

Note: Locators in *italic* refer to figures, and bold refer to tables.

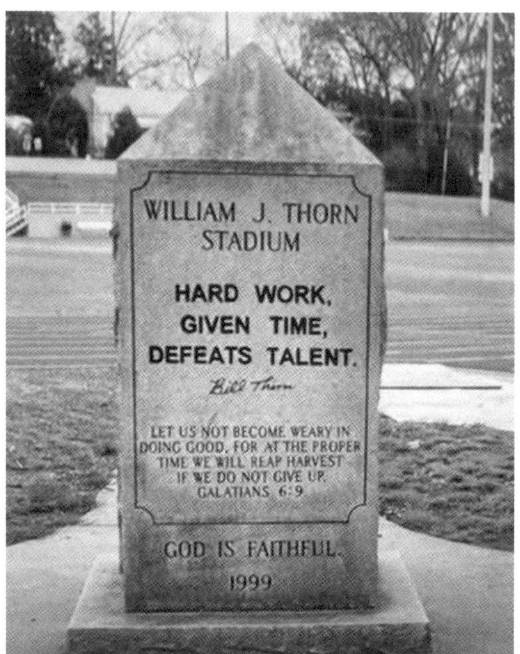

Thorn Stadium

ABOUT THE AUTHOR

THE JOSHUA GROUP CONSULTING, founded in 2007 and located in a suburb of Atlanta, Georgia, is a boutique business consulting and leadership coaching company. The Joshua Group is dedicated to helping individuals and organizations "do what they do, better." Drawing from a rich heritage of builders—ranging from sculptors to home builders—the firm channels this legacy into constructing stronger leaders, teams, and systems. Their services encompass executive coaching, leadership training, team development workshops, business consulting, and sales and marketing consulting, all tailored to the unique needs and cultures of their clients.

The Joshua Group is comprised of a diverse team of experts, including coaches, trainers, consultants, and storytellers. This team is committed to building not just better businesses, but better people. Their approach is deeply rooted in principles of servant leadership, integrity, and continuous improvement. By focusing on personalized development and fostering environments of trust and accountability, The Joshua Group empowers clients to achieve lasting transformation and success.

The Joshua Group's insights and methodologies provided a foundational framework for understanding and applying the leadership lessons derived from Coach Bill Thorn's life. Their emphasis on building from the inside out aligns seamlessly with the values and principles that Coach Thorn exemplified throughout his career.

This is the group's first published book. For more information about The Joshua Group, please visit the company's website at www.thejoshuagroup.net.

For additional photos, stories, and videos of Bill Thorn's life, please visit us at www.CoachBillThorn.com.